T0099380

If These WALLS Could TALK:
OHIO STATE BUCKEYES

Stories from the
Ohio State Buckeyes Sideline,
Locker Room, and Press Box

Paul Keels

with Zack Meisel

TRIUMPH
BOOKS

Copyright © 2018 by Paul Keels and Zack Meisel

No part of this publication may be reproduced, stored in a retrieval system, or transmitted in any form by any means, electronic, mechanical, photocopying, or otherwise, without the prior written permission of the publisher, Triumph Books LLC, 814 North Franklin Street, Chicago, Illinois 60610.

Library of Congress Cataloguing-in-Publication Data available upon request

This book is available in quantity at special discounts for your group or organization. For further information, contact:

Triumph Books LLC
814 North Franklin Street
Chicago, Illinois 60610
(312) 337–0747
www.triumphbooks.com

Printed in U.S.A.
ISBN: 978-1-62937-624-0
Design by Amy Carter
Editorial production by Alex Lubertozzi
Photos courtesy of AP Images unless otherwise indicated

To Buckeye fans everywhere! Your passion gives us purpose!

CONTENTS

FOREWORD

by Thad Matta

On the night of July 5, 2004, I remember calling Andy Geiger at 11:00 PM to inform him that I was withdrawing from Ohio State University's search for a new head basketball coach.

The situation at Xavier had gotten completely out of hand with regard to media speculation about my candidacy. As I told Andy of my decision, he stopped me and said, "I am sitting on a gold mine up here. I need you to come help me mine it."

I asked him, "Are you offering me the job?"

His response is what changed my mind. He told me, "If you come up here and screw up the interview, I will give you two hours to publicly withdraw your name."

I said, "Fair enough. I will see you in the morning." From the moment the press conference ended around 2:00 PM on July 8, it was game on.

I knew there were major obstacles that would have to be overcome in terms of NCAA sanctions that would be handed down to the university from what had transpired prior to my arrival. What I didn't realize was that Ohio State basketball had never quite sustained success throughout the program's history. Three consecutive NCAA Tournament appearances constituted the longest successful streak, and that dated back to 1960.

But the major statistic that really grabbed me was the program's winning percentage of 51 percent in the history of Big Ten play. As I have found out, anytime you take a new job, the real truth of the situation never comes out until you have begun the journey. I remember coming off of the recruiting trail for a few hours to meet with my new support staff. My first meeting was with Miechelle Willis, senior associate athletic director, the person to whom I would report. The meeting was to give me a briefing and background on the players who were currently in the program. At the conclusion of that meeting, I sat there dumbfounded. As Miechelle left, I remember thinking of one of my all-time favorite movies, *The Dirty Dozen*. The immediate goal became to change the culture and environment in which our guys would operate on a daily basis.

As I have said publicly any chance I ever got, Brandon Fuss-Cheatham, Tony Stockman, Matt Sylvester, Terence Dials, Je'Kel Foster, J.J. Sullinger, Matt Marinchick—they should all have their names hanging from the rafters of the Schottenstein Center. Those first two teams were the unsung heroes of my 13-year career at Ohio State. From upsetting an undefeated and No. 1–ranked Illinois team on Senior Day, to winning the Big Ten Championship in Year 2, they proved to be a collection of guys who bought in to loving each other, the university, and the process.

From that point forward came some of the greatest players and teams to ever wear the scarlet and gray. We won a number of Big Ten championships as well as conference tournament championships and we went to two Final Fours. There were All-Americans, a National Player of the Year, National Defenders of the Year, Academic All-Americans, a National Freshman of the Year as well as a supporting cast on each team that did more for the program than anybody will ever know.

Toward the end of my tenure at Ohio State, we had what I have often described as an extended run of bad luck. We lost key guys to injuries and we battled team issues that hadn't been present in the prior years. That said, I take full responsibility for what happened to the program in my final years. What I am most proud of, as I look back now over my tenure, is that in the current circumstances that surround college basketball, our program was run the right way.

Finally, I want to touch on my relationship with Paul Keels. I would be lying if I said I ever enjoyed spending time in front of the media. However, if I could pick one person to be interviewed by, it would be Paul. He was always prepared, knowledgeable, and living in the moment. I have never dealt with a person in his position who cared more than he did. You have to realize that he was with me at the highest of the highs and the lowest of the lows. He knew when I was hurting and he always showed sincere compassion. And when I was happy, there was no greater friend with whom to share the moment.

Thanks for all of the softballs, Paul!

—Thad Matta

FOREWORD

by Jim Lachey

My first experience with Ohio State football happened in 1968, when I was five years old, listening to the Buckeyes on the radio as they played in the Rose Bowl. The team had just captured the national championship with the help of a fullback from Celina, Ohio, named Jim Otis.

My hometown, St. Henry, about 10 miles south of Celina, didn't have football at our school at the time, so there really wasn't a high school team to follow. Naturally, we jumped on the Buckeyes bandwagon, and I have never left. St. Henry started a team in 1973, and eight years later, I was offered a scholarship to Ohio State.

Playing for the scarlet and gray is every Ohio state high school football player's dream, and mine came true. Woody Hayes came to see me play high school football, and soon after, Earle Bruce told me he wanted me to be a Buckeye. During the recruiting process, while I was visiting other schools and watching them play football, the public address announcer would provide scores from games around the country. I was always just interested in what the Buckeyes were doing. A lot of times, I would think, *What am I doing here? I want to be a Buckeye.*

I had four great years at Ohio State, where I ended up being an All-American offensive guard. I was drafted to the NFL in the first round to the San Diego Chargers. After an 11-year career in the NFL and a Super Bowl championship with the Washington Redskins, I retired from playing football after the 1995 season. Shortly after, I got the opportunity of a lifetime: to be the color analyst for the Ohio State Radio Network.

Truthfully, I didn't really know much about the broadcasting end, but I was very confident in my ability to talk football. After working the 1997 season with talented play-by-play announcer Terry Smith, he left for the California Angels play-by-play job. The Ohio State network was seeking a replacement. It was a highly sought-after job, and many applied from all over the country.

The decision was made, and I was informed we had hired Paul Keels from the Cincinnati Bearcats Radio Network. He was a legend in Cincinnati. Paul grew up there, went to Cincinnati Moeller High School, then Xavier University, and the whole time, he was involved in student radio stations, broadcasting football games and other sports.

I was excited because I had heard him call Bearcats games in the past, but I never had the chance to meet him. The first time we met was in July 1998, when we played golf at Ohio State before the football season began. I think we both knew this was going to work and that, hopefully, we would have some fun along the way. We are now in our 21st year working together and, yes, we are still having a blast.

It all started with the 1998 season opener on the road against West Virginia. It was Paul's first Ohio State football game, and the Buckeyes won 34–17. Paul was great! I think in about five hours of broadcasting that day, he made only one mistake. When describing the uniforms while announcing the starting lineups, he mentioned red trim on the players' pants. I quickly mentioned that we like to call that "scarlet" around here. From then on, it was scarlet.

Paul was a professional all the way. We have had the opportunity to follow the Buckeyes teams led by John Cooper, Jim Tressel, Luke Fickell, and now Urban Meyer. What a ride it's been. Certainly, the 2002 national championship game against Miami will always be considered one of the greatest ever. The Hurricanes had a 34-game winning streak and a roster full of future NFL stars. The Buckeyes fought, scratched, and clawed their way to a double-overtime victory. I will never forget, long after the game, walking with Paul and the crew from Sun Devil Stadium to the parking garage. There was not much talking until we got to the car. We were all stunned and looked at each other and started laughing, screaming, and we even had a few tears of joy.

The 2014 national championship run got interesting when Braxton Miller was lost for the season and then J.T. Barrett got hurt in the second half against That Team Up North, and Cardale Jones took over. Certainly, the game against Alabama is one Paul and I will never forget.

The Buckeyes barely made the playoffs and then had to face the Crimson Tide and Nick Saban. Down 21–3, it looked like the season was over. But then the turnovers stopped and the field goals started to turn into touchdown drives. The turning point was the touchdown before halftime, when Evan Spencer completed a pass to Michael Thomas, who tiptoed the end zone sideline to make an incredible catch and bring the Buckeyes to within one point.

I looked at Paul and said, "We've got them right where we want them."

In the second half, Ohio State dominated on the line of scrimmage on both sides of the ball and wore them out with Ezekiel Elliott.

Those two seasons are highlights of many great years working with Paul as we share Buckeyes football with our loyal listeners. I can't forget to mention the dominance the Buckeyes have had over That Team Up North the last 21 years, in which the Buckeyes have won 16 times. Paul and I have had a bird's-eye view of every game, and his ability to share what he sees is one of a kind.

—Jim Lachey

INTRODUCTION

20 YEARS IN THE MAKING

Editor's note: Paul Keels' direct quotes are highlighted throughout the book.

Paul Keels was a wide-eyed sophomore in high school, filing into Ohio Stadium for the first time in 1972 with his grandfather.

He wasn't there for one of Woody and Bo's classic battles during the fabled Ten-Year War. This wasn't an overcast Saturday afternoon in the fall, with the vibrant leaves matching the scarlet on the Buckeyes' uniforms. No, this was a preseason clash between the Cleveland Browns and Cincinnati Bengals. Okay, *clash* might be a bit strong. This was an exhibition contest, an event at the Horseshoe with discounted fanfare and intrigue. Robert Dorsey, a friend of Keels' parents, had played on the offensive line at Ohio State in the 1940s. He gifted tickets for the game to Keels' grandfather, who lived in Columbus.

The Browns and Bengals met in Columbus in the preseason for three consecutive years from 1972 to 1974. The Browns won two of the three Sunday matinees—Keels witnessed the Bengals' lone victory, a 27–21 triumph—but fans in attendance dismissed traditional rooting practices and instead cheered for whichever former Buckeyes were playing for either team.

Keels can remember peering up at the state highway patrolmen standing on the top corners of the venue, monitoring every movement. He can recall being overwhelmed by the sheer size of the legendary football cathedral, constructed in 1922 and growing larger ever since. He had watched some Ohio State games on TV. He had listened to the action on the radio. But the stark realization of seeing the Horseshoe in person made an impression. Little did he know just how impactful that experience would be.

Keels was tackled on the Ohio Stadium grass for the first time— well, the only time—in 1974. When he was a senior at Cincinnati Moeller High School, the football team opposed Warren Harding in a playoff game in Columbus. Keels joined a group of friends who rode a bus north on I-71 to attend the affair. Toward the end of halftime, a horde of students paraded down to the field—where the home team now

enters from the southeast tunnel—
to form a passageway for the team
as it exited the locker room. After
the players rushed back onto the
field, Keels and his friends headed
up toward their seats. But one of
his buddies ran up from behind
and planted him in the grass.

Archie Griffin, Eddie George,
Chic Harley, Hopalong Cassady,
Troy Smith, Paul Keels—they

Paul Keels

have all been knocked to the ground at Ohio Stadium.

Keels has since been involved in countless memorable moments
at the stadium, especially in the last 20 years, when he has served as
the voice of the Buckeyes. His calming baritone has chronicled a pair
of Ohio State football championships, a trio of marches to the Final
Four in men's basketball, and an ever-growing list of unforgettable
passes, catches, runs, three-pointers, and defensive stops. He has forged
bonds with some of the most prominent coaches in both sports and has
detailed some of the greatest athletes' signature moments to those listening intently to the broadcasts.

Keels was raised in Cincinnati. He attended Xavier University,
where he studied communications. After high school, he did not return
to Ohio Stadium until 1982, when the Buckeyes hosted Michigan in the
annual meeting between the Big Ten rivals. He worked for WWJ radio
in Detroit, one of five stations to carry Michigan football games each
Saturday in the fall.

*That was strange, when I would come down from Detroit,
back into my home state.*

He followed Ohio State football as a kid. His mother attended Ohio State. His grandparents and other relatives lived in the area. But in the 1980s, he arrived in Columbus every other year with Ohio State's sworn enemy. Keels returned to Cincinnati and served as the radio voice for University of Cincinnati games. He also called Bengals games on the radio for one year before his network lost the contractual rights. He later called Bengals preseason contests.

In 1998 he was offered the Ohio State broadcasting gig. He struggled with the decision at first. He lived in his hometown. He enjoyed his job. He was in the process of selling his house. This wasn't easy. Keels was filling in for a Cincinnati Reds series in San Diego that June. He told the employer he would reveal his decision when he returned from the sun-splashed West Coast trip.

I realized that neither choice was going to be a bad choice, but something like doing Ohio State was a once-in-a-lifetime thing, and I'd probably regret it if I didn't jump on it. It was obviously a good move for me.

Keels was the prototypical sports-obsessed kid growing up in Cincinnati. He wasn't equipped with the skill to play any sports at a notable level, but he closely followed the NBA's Cincinnati Royals, at least until they relocated to Kansas City in 1972. He also followed the Reds and the football and basketball teams at the University of Cincinnati and at Xavier.

He cherished the times he listened to the radio at home with his parents, as Jim McIntyre and Joe Nuxhall set the scene at Crosley Field. His father took him and his brother to a Reds game once and introduced him to McIntyre.

"Hey," his father said, "this is one of the guys you listen to when you listen to games on the radio at night."

Keels still calls upon that memory when he meets Ohio State fans and their children. He can remember when a little-known announcer named Al Michaels, who had been calling games of the minor league Hawaii Islanders of the Pacific Coast League, replaced McIntyre in the Reds' booth. Marty Brennaman assumed Michaels' position three years later. Keels ended up working with both Brennaman and Nuxhall a couple of times in the late 1990s.

Without seeing it himself, he could describe the Cincinnati Gardens and could picture Nate "Tiny" Archibald scoring and dishing out assists at will. Keels used to bug Royals radio announcer Dom Valentino for autographs at the end of games. Those memories fueled his desire to become involved with the student radio station at Xavier. There, he called high school and college games, the genesis of what would evolve into a decades-long career in the industry.

I always felt it was the guys on the radio who connected you to the teams and the players that you followed. I wanted to be that connection. Not so much for the recognition, but just to connect people who follow a team or tune in to an event that means a lot to them.

Keels had to wait two weeks to announce his job switch once he gave his notice to WLW in Cincinnati in 1998. During that time, Ohio State and Cincinnati struck an agreement to play multiple times in the coming years.

In that two-week period, friends and family members would tell him, "Oh, isn't that great? You're going to get to do a game at Ohio Stadium!" Keels had to keep quiet. He could not reveal his secret just yet, so he would simply smile and politely nod.

But what he really wanted to say was, "Well, I'm going to get to do more than one."

CHAPTER 1

1998—AN EVENTFUL ROOKIE YEAR

John Cooper had presided over the Ohio State football program for a decade when Paul Keels started his gig in Columbus in 1998. With Cooper at the helm, Keels (and broadcast partner Jim Lachey) had access to the team's closed practices, where he met coaches and former players, including two-time Heisman Trophy winner Archie Griffin.

The Buckeyes were ranked No. 1 in the country to start the season. Cooper had recruited all-world talent at virtually every position on the field. They returned senior quarterback Joe Germaine. Linebacker Jerry Rudzinski and cornerback Antoine Winfield anchored the Silver Bullets on defense.

Ohio State had been ranked in the top four at some point in each of the three previous seasons, but that maize-and-blue thorn in their side kept derailing things in late November.

This was the year to put it all together, the first year of the BCS system. The Buckeyes were oozing talent on both sides of the ball. Cooper ran the program like a CEO. Keels can remember attending practices and hearing assistant coaches doing the yelling and the instructing. They were the loud ones, the intense ones. He can still hear Jon Tenuta, Tim Spencer, and Fred Pagac shouting today. Spencer, the running backs coach, looked like he could still carry the ball and evade some tackles.

Meanwhile, Cooper wandered the field, hopping from position group to position group and making the occasional pit stop to talk to some visitors on the sideline.

The Buckeyes began the season with a road game at West Virginia, a marquee matchup in Morgantown on a Saturday night in the first week of September. The Mountaineers, behind quarterback Marc Bulger—an eventual two-time Pro Bowler with the St. Louis Rams—and running back Amos Zereoue—who played for seven years in the NFL—owned the No. 11 ranking in the nation.

Keels had traveled to Morgantown in the past, since Cincinnati played West Virginia on occasion. He drove to the campus for West

Virginia's media day so he could familiarize himself with members of the Mountaineers' staff and roster. There, he interviewed a few players and head coach Don Nehlen.

Keels and the rest of the broadcast crew drove to West Virginia early that Saturday afternoon for the opener. While Ohio State's players and coaches were focused on the pivotal game, Keels was wondering what it would be like to work with a different group of people on a grander stage. How would everything flow? Where would everyone be positioned? Would they be accommodating to him? Would it be a seamless transition? Producers were giving him hand signals and other directions that were a bit confusing, a bit different from what he was accustomed to at his previous gig. During the first commercial, he told them to hold off on the procedures, that they could figure things out and get comfortable with each other as they went along.

From there, he was able to fixate on the game. And West Virginia was charged up to host the top-ranked team in the country.

There was a buzz around the stadium.

It didn't last.

The last University of Cincinnati basketball game Keels called came against West Virginia in the second round of the NCAA Tournament in March 1998. The No. 2 seed Bearcats met the No. 10 seed Mountaineers at Taco Bell Arena in Boise, Idaho (the same building in which the Buckeyes' men's basketball team played its two NCAA Tournament games in March 2018). D'Juan Baker nailed a three-pointer with seven seconds left to hand Cincinnati a 74–72 advantage, but West Virginia's Jarrod West answered with a definitive three-pointer off the glass with 0.8 seconds remaining.

So when Keels ran into Tony Caridi, West Virginia's radio broadcaster, six months later at Mountaineer Field, Caridi said: "Last time we saw you, your team lost to the Mountaineers. Maybe it'll work out this day."

Plenty of Buckeyes supporters made the trek from Columbus. The crowd of 68,409 is the third-largest in the venue's history. Ohio State won the game 34–17, without too much trouble. Joe Germaine, the senior quarterback and co-captain, threw for 301 yards and two touchdowns. Michael Wiley rushed 17 times for 140 yards and a score. It would be the closest game they'd play until early November, as they continued to clutch the No. 1 ranking until their November 7 matchup against Michigan State at Ohio Stadium. The Buckeyes blasted their first eight opponents by an average of 29 points per game.

"In my opinion, that 1998 team was one of the best teams to ever play college football," said running back Jonathan Wells. "We were very explosive."

Then came Black Saturday.

The Buckeyes were a 28-point favorite on November 7, 1998. They carried a 24–9 lead in the third quarter. Michigan State head coach Nick Saban told his team to prepare for a 15-round fight and "to be Rocky in that 15th round." The Buckeyes couldn't get back to their feet after the Spartans delivered a knockout punch in the fourth quarter for the TKO heard 'round the nation. Five Buckeyes turnovers spoiled what should have been a serene Saturday afternoon at the 'Shoe. Instead, a team that Saban described as "the squirts in the neighborhood who had to pick a fight with the bully" rattled off 19 unanswered points to slam the door shut on Ohio State's title hopes.

In November 2015 Wiley and former offensive tackle Orlando Pace watched another shocking Ohio State loss to Michigan State at the Columbus home of former receiver Dee Miller. The three played together under Cooper in the late '90s. Pace, now a member of both the College Football Hall of Fame and Pro Football Hall of Fame, routinely flattened defensive linemen and hapless pass rushers. He created gaping holes for Wiley and other ball carriers, and he bought time for Ohio State's quarterbacks so they could sling the ball downfield to Miller.

Pace had departed for the NFL before Ohio State hosted Michigan State in 1998, but his buddies saw the field in Columbus that day. As the trio watched Mark Dantonio's squad rewrite that script 17 years later, they reflected on that miserable afternoon in 1998.

"Aw, Mill, I was so sick when you all lost it," said Pace, the No. 1 overall draft selection in 1998.

"How did we let that slip through our hands?" Wiley asked.

In 2015 a similar story unfolded. The Buckeyes, the reigning champions, appeared destined for a second straight College Football Playoff berth. And then, a seemingly overmatched Michigan State team, missing its starting quarterback and playing on the road, dashed those dreams.

"Sometimes…at Ohio State, it's like, 'Who can beat us in this conference?'" Miller said. "'We're going to show up and we're going to be wearing the scarlet and gray, and on paper we know we're better than this team.' And at the end of the game, you're on the losing end, and you're like, 'Man, did this really happen?' And it kind of wakes you up. It was really difficult, to be honest. We knew that we had lost a really, really special opportunity. We all come in every preseason wanting to win the national title game. You look at your Ohio States, Florida States, Alabamas, and it's almost sad to say that anything less than a national championship is not really good. You have your coaches who are paid $5–6 million. You're coming in with the best recruiting classes. So everybody expects you to get to the top."

Bill Burke, a graduate of Howland High School in Warren, Ohio, directed Michigan State to the upset in 1998. He had been named the Northeast Ohio Division II Player of the Year in 1994, but he ended up in enemy territory for college.

"I think it was somewhat of a panic by everybody," Miller said.

Germaine, under duress, hurried a pass toward Miller in the end zone on the Buckeyes' final play. Michigan State defensive back Renaldo Hill stepped in front, intercepted the pass, and sealed the 28–24 upset.

Ohio native Bill Burke, the Spartans' starting quarterback, celebrates the Spartans' 28–24 victory over the Buckeyes on November 7, 1998. *Photo courtesy of Getty Images*

Years later, Miller's wide receivers coach with the Green Bay Packers, Charlie Baggett—who served as an assistant under Saban at Michigan State—told Miller that the Spartans knew the exact route he was going to run on Ohio State's last attempt. That added salt to Miller's wound.

"Maybe if it wasn't me they threw the ball to on the last play, I'd be like, 'Oh, well. We lost,'" Miller said. "But, no, I'm somewhat responsible for not making the play that we needed to make to stay undefeated and ranked No. 1."

Instead, it still eats at Miller today. Any reminder of Michigan State bothers him, including the school's colors. (Don't mention to him that he had to wear the renowned hues of the Green Bay Packers, who selected him in the sixth round of the 1999 NFL Draft.) "Man, I hate green," he said. "I hate green. My wife will get me socks to wear with my suits, and if they have any green on them, I'll be like, 'Take those socks back.' I never wear green. I wish they would change the color of money."

In December 2013, a few days before Michigan State again wrecked Ohio State's national championship chances, a friend texted Miller a picture from that 1998 letdown. It happened to be Miller's birthday. "I'm like, 'Dude, you just messed up my birthday,'" Miller said. "I can't block it out. Just that whole sequence, that whole drive. I'll never be able to block that out."

There was a somber atmosphere in the locker room after the game. Miller said it was like somebody had died. Keels said he remembers "a stunned silence."

"It was ugly," Wells said. "When you know that you're better than somebody, but unfortunately, on that day, they're better than you, you have to just live with it. It's a tough pill to swallow. It was tough. We were very disappointed. We were heartbroken. We had shown no signs of being beatable that season."

Neither Wells nor Miller has ever gone back and rewatched that game. Miller said he'll receive texts informing him that he's on the Big Ten Network when the broadcast re-airs, which irks him. "People think it's cool that you're on TV," he said, "but you're on TV for the wrong damn reason. I have never watched that game. Even the next day, watching it on film just made me sick to my stomach. Here we are with all of this firepower, being ranked No. 1. That was the first year of the BCS, so we found out that our mess-up let everyone know that if you lose, you better lose early in the season. If you lose at the end of the season, there's no way for you to get back into that national championship hunt."

Even Cooper admitted as much. After the stunning loss, he said, "Realistically, I don't think we have a chance of winning the national championship. A lot of things would need to happen, and I don't have a clue how far we'll drop."

The answer? Ohio State tumbled six spots, to No. 7 in the nation. Another crushing November defeat, only this time to the *other* team in Michigan. Perhaps the Buckeyes' reputation would have developed differently had they lost to, say, West Virginia in the opener, instead of Michigan State in November, with the bowl picture coming into focus.

I think it left people wondering, "Okay, what's going to happen next? Can they still win the Big Ten?" Had they lost to West Virginia earlier in the year, at least it was on the road, it was a team that had been ranked. Or, as difficult as it might have been, had they lost to Michigan at the end of the year, at least they'd seen that movie before. Had they lost in the BCS Championship Game, well, at least they got there. That was one that caught everybody off-guard, because it seemingly came out of nowhere.

The next week, a peeved Ohio State team walloped Iowa 45–14. The week after that, they conquered Michigan 31–16, tied for the second-largest margin of victory over their nemesis in 30 years. It was Cooper's second and final victory against Michigan. "We were like, 'Man, we can't lose this game after basically losing the national championship,'" Miller said. "So, it was just trying to get back and focused."

Ohio State's consolation prize was a date with Texas A&M in the Sugar Bowl. The Buckeyes, ranked third in the country, bested the No. 8 Aggies 24–14. "Even though we won the Big Ten and we beat Texas A&M," Miller said, "we did not win the national championship and we felt like we were one of the best teams that ever came to Ohio State. It was just that one game. I never want anyone to feel what I felt."

Other teams would. The Spartans thwarted Ohio State's bid for a national title game berth in 2013. Michigan State gashed Ohio State's defense, dashed Ohio State's championship dreams, and crashed what appeared to be an inevitable clash between Florida State and Ohio State at the Rose Bowl. Mark Dantonio's crew upset the unbeaten Buckeyes 34–24 in the Big Ten Championship Game at Lucas Oil Stadium in Indianapolis. Instead of a trip to Pasadena, the Buckeyes had to settle for a flight to South Beach, where they lost to Clemson in the Orange Bowl.

Two years later, Michigan State turned the trick again with a 41-yard field goal as time expired. The Spartans erased No. 2 Ohio State's unblemished record a week before the Michigan game with a 17–14 final score. Michigan State was without starting quarterback Connor Cook, which only added salt to the wound.

A couple of different times over the last 20 years, Michigan State has ruined some of their dreams.

Jim Tressel asked Miller to speak to the team before its expedition to East Lansing, Michigan, in October 2006. The Buckeyes proceeded to smack around the Spartans 38–7. And yet, Miller remained dissatisfied. "I still didn't feel any type of payback feeling," Miller said. "We won as a university, but I wasn't like, 'Yeah, now take that!' I really feel like there's nothing anyone can do to make me feel like it's payback."

The 1998 wound remains fresh for those who endured it. That game seemed to spark the downward spiral of Cooper's tenure in Columbus. The following year, Ohio State finished 6–6 and did not participate in bowl season. They dropped their final three games, with a lackluster effort in a 23–7 loss at Michigan State, a 46–20 drubbing by Illinois at home and then another failure at Michigan, with a 24–17 loss. There was some hope entering that game in Ann Arbor that a victory could vault the Buckeyes to the Motor City Bowl at the Pontiac Silverdome. That provided a particularly peculiar perspective for Keels. He had called University of Cincinnati football games for a long time, and in his final year in that position, the Bearcats reached their first bowl game in 47 years. He can recall how thrilled those affiliated with the program and the fan base were that Cincinnati had been selected to play in the Humanitarian Bowl (in which it defeated Utah State 35–19). In his second year on the Ohio State radio broadcast, the Buckeyes did not appear in a bowl game, conveying to him the other end of the disposition spectrum.

The 2000 season proved to be Cooper's last at the helm. The Buckeyes were 8–3 heading into the Outback Bowl, where they squared off against South Carolina and head coach Lou Holtz, an assistant coach under Woody Hayes on Ohio State's 1968 national championship team, and running back Ryan Brewer, a native of Troy, Ohio. The day before the game in Tampa, Keels met with Cooper in the coach's hotel room to record a pregame interview. Cooper and his wife, Helen, and another couple were getting ready to head to dinner. Cooper introduced Keels to everyone and asked if he wanted to sit and have a drink. Keels politely declined and marveled at the idea that Cooper could be so calm and so courteous given that, if the Outback Bowl didn't unfold in his favor, he could very well find himself on the unemployment line.

Ohio State lost to South Carolina 24–7, with Brewer being named the game's MVP for his three-touchdown performance. After the game, Keels sat in the team hotel, as Ohio State's charter flight home was delayed. He was sitting with coworkers and athletic director Andy Geiger, who seemed to be visibly wrestling with the entire situation. Did a coaching change need to be made? Was the time right? Did Cooper deserve another year? Geiger chose his words carefully when speaking with Keels at the hotel. Sure enough, Cooper was fired the next day.

In a press conference following his dismissal, Cooper noted his 3–8 record in bowl games. He expressed that he had hoped he could hang onto his job for at least one more season. Geiger called the Outback Bowl shortcoming "a capstone on what we have seen as a deteriorating climate within the football program." Geiger cited concern about player discipline and academic motivation and overall team competitiveness as factors in his decision, and he painted the South Carolina loss as an all-encompassing portrait of the program's problems. Cooper finished with more wins in school history than any coach not named Woody Hayes, but he also finished with a 2–10–1 record against Michigan.

A few weeks after Cooper's exit, Keels called his house phone and left him a message. Cooper returned the call. The two thanked each other for making each other's jobs a bit easier.

For a new guy coming into a job like that, it couldn't have been better. If they don't lose that game to Michigan State in 1998, they get to the BCS Championship, and they're probably playing Tennessee for the title. That Ohio State team had so much talent on both sides of the ball. You liked their chances to win that championship. And if they do, how much longer is Cooper the head coach? I can see why that game would stick out to some of those guys. If they don't lose that Michigan State game, they at least get to a BCS Championship, and Cooper's coaching at least another couple of years.

ARCHIE AND ME

by Paul Keels

My first introduction to Archie Griffin was via the radio. While working a part-time job during my high school years, I had a transistor AM radio with an earplug. The radio was usually tuned to whatever sporting events were on the air. On Saturdays, that would be whatever college football games the radio would pick up, and the majority of the time, that would be the Ohio State game. Marv Homan was the announcer for the broadcasts that were carried in Cincinnati, and it always caught my attention when I heard the name of a player either from the Queen City or from Moeller High School, where I was a student.

So it was through the radio that I became familiar with this uber-talented Ohio State freshman who would run wild on the rest of the Big Ten. My part-time job also helped to educate me—I was delivering the afternoon editions of the now-defunct *Cincinnati Post and Times-Star*. Their sports page was an important piece for my education of what was happening in the sports world, and the success of the Buckeyes was a regular feature, especially given the presence of local players on the Ohio State roster.

At that time, in the 1970s, only a few Ohio State games would air on TV: the Ohio State–Michigan game, maybe one other regular season contest, and the Rose Bowl. Those helped me learn more about the great running back who would make history by twice claiming the Heisman Trophy.

Then the legend of Archie Griffin came closer to home. The Cincinnati Bengals made Archie their first-round draft pick in 1976. He immediately grabbed headlines and attention. While in college at Xavier University, our student station broadcast Friday night high school football games. On one late fall Friday night, I was part of a student group calling a game at Riverfront Stadium. It was an exciting opportunity to be working a game in a professional stadium in a real press box.

Meanwhile, in the booth right next to our setup was a Cincinnati commercial station that also aired high school games each weekend. Their announcer was a man named Bill Meredith, with whom I became better acquainted over the coming years. Bill was always willing to help provide information to us aspiring broadcasters. As kickoff approached, we noticed that Bill had a guest analyst in the booth with him that night, none other than Bengals running back Archie Griffin.

As dumb as it sounds, it was a thrill for us college kids to just be near someone who had already achieved such legendary status. I never had a chance to meet Archie that night. Instead, that would come many years later, after I moved to Columbus. When I took the job as Ohio State's radio announcer in 1998, Archie was still a member of the athletic department.

Archie Griffin (45) runs for some of his 163 yards in a 10–10 tie against the Michigan Wolverines in Ann Arbor on November 24, 1973.

Upon meeting him, there were a couple of things that became quite clear:

1. Given the opportunity, chatting with Archie about the Bengals was a surefire icebreaker. It helped that I had spent years broadcasting Bengals preseason games on TV.
2. He was genuinely nice, and people treated him as if he were just a few days removed from winning his pair of Heisman Trophies.

Over the years, I have met and interviewed Archie on a number of occasions. Most notably, on September 10, 2016, Ohio State hosted Tulsa at the Horseshoe, and there was a lengthy lightning delay. While we were figuring out how to handle all of the unfilled air time that the delay caused, Archie walked over to our radio booth from the suite next door and spent a considerable amount of time on the air discussing numerous subjects.

It was also a thrill during the 1999 football season to watch Archie be honored on the field at halftime of a game. His No. 45 was the first Ohio State football number to be officially retired. School officials concocted a reason that Archie needed to be on the field during halftime. Members of his family, meanwhile, had been secretly let in on the act. Archie had no idea what was to come. It was a great, deserving honor for a guy who had presented Ohio State fans with so many thrills on the field.

I still have an Archie Griffin Bengals rookie card. Every now and then I tell him, "Archie, one of these days, I have to get you to sign it for me." It really is an amazing thing, that every so often you have to pinch yourself and say, "You've gotten a chance to be around and socialize with people who have meant so much to this program and to these fans."

CHAPTER 2
A FINAL FOUR
APPEARANCE
NO ONE SAW COMING

Years ago, Paul Keels was invited to a fish fry at a watering hole on the east side of Columbus by David Barker, a member of the 1960 Ohio State men's basketball team. There, he met Mel Nowell, one of Barker's teammates, and a number of other former Buckeyes hoopsters, and he learned that the particular location for the event was selected because of its affinity for the basketball program. When he scanned the walls of the bar, he noticed rows of Ohio State basketball photos. There was no evidence that a Columbus-based football team even existed. There might not be another such location in central Ohio.

While there is no denial that football drives the bus for Ohio State athletics in so many ways, once you become exposed to the tradition of Buckeyes men's basketball, it is very easy to understand its importance to those who have been a part of it and those who loyally follow and support it. While the football program boasts multiple national titles, the 1960 NCAA Tournament title claimed by coach Fred Taylor and those who played for him holds a special place for so many, maybe because it is the first and only. Following the 1960 title season, for a number of years, Ohio State basketball, by many casual observers' accounts, was something to occupy Buckeyes sports fans between football seasons.

There was Gary Bradds' scoring rampage in 1964, when the senior forward scored 40 or more points in six consecutive games, including a program-record 49 against Illinois on February 10. Bradds holds four of the top six single-game scoring marks in school history. Basketball fever spread around town when the 1968 Buckeyes reached the Final Four on the backs of Bill Hosket, Steve Howell, and Dave Sorenson, with an 82–81 win against Kentucky in Lexington, a challenge one former player referred to as the UK Invitational. Eldon Miller took over for Taylor and directed the team to a handful of NCAA Tournament appearances in the 1980s, as he coached such talents as Clark Kellogg, Herb Williams, Kelvin Ransey, Dennis Hopson, Tony Campbell, and the Canton-born backcourt duo of Troy Taylor and Ron Stokes.

The 1991–92 team reached the regional final, where it sputtered against Michigan and its famed Fab Five. That Buckeyes team, behind Jim Jackson, Chris Jent, and Lawrence Funderburke, had finished first in the Big Ten standings. A rough stretch ensued, and the basketball program dropped to new depths.

By 1999, the pieces were in place, even if it required some contact lenses and a microscope to see the potential. When Paul Keels relocated to Columbus in 1998, the Ohio State men's basketball program had little influence. The Buckeyes had stumbled through an 8–22 season in Jim O'Brien's first year at the helm. They posted a 1–15 record in Big Ten play, the doormat of the 11-team league. The team had not registered a winning season since 1993, when it went 15–13.

Football was king, a national and perennial powerhouse program under John Cooper (you know, so long as they could slip past that pesky rival Michigan). Basketball barely registered a ripple on the town's excitement meter.

For Keels, it was a bit of a reversal from the norm. In his final year calling Cincinnati Bearcats games, the football team reached its first bowl game in 47 years—toppling Utah State in the inaugural Humanitarian Bowl, 35–19, in Boise, Idaho. The basketball program, on the other hand, was flourishing under the direction of Bob Huggins. The Bearcats racked up a 27–6 record (including 14–2 in Conference USA play) during the 1997–98 season. They entered the NCAA Tournament as a No. 2 seed, though they slipped up against No. 10 West Virginia with a Sweet 16 berth on the line, as Jarrod West's last-gasp, off-the-glass three-pointer sank Cincinnati. The Bearcats had a couple of future long-term NBA players on their roster in Kenyon Martin and Ruben Patterson. The year before, anchored by junior forward Danny Fortson, Cincinnati amassed a 26–8 record and earned a No. 3 seed in the NCAA Tournament. In fact, consider what Keels had grown accustomed to during his time in southwest Ohio:

1997–98 27–6 overall (14–2 in Conference USA play)

1996–97 26–8 overall (12–2 in Conference USA play)

1995–96 28–5 overall (11–3 in Conference USA play, reached Elite Eight)

1994–95 22–12 overall (7–5 in Great Midwest Conference play)

1993–94 22–10 overall (7–5 in Great Midwest Conference play)

1992–93 27–5 overall (8–2 in Great Midwest Conference play, reached Elite Eight)

1991–92 29–5 overall (8–2 in Great Midwest Conference play, reached Final Four)

So when Keels took over as play-by-play announcer at Ohio State, he began his research into the basketball program. The task should have been accompanied by a "Do Not Try This at Home" warning. The findings were horrifying. Just take a glance at Ohio State's records in prior seasons.

1997–98 8–22 overall (1–15 in Big Ten play)

1996–97 10–17 overall (5–13 in Big Ten play)

1995–96 10–17 overall (3–15 in Big Ten play)

1994–95 6–22 overall (2–16 in Big Ten play)

1993–94 13–16 overall (6–12 in Big Ten play)

The 1994–95 campaign included a tour of losses around the Buckeye State. Randy Ayers' bunch fell by 11 points to Ohio University at home, by two points at Cleveland State, and by nine points to Bowling Green at St. John Arena in non-conference competition. That team also lost by 20 to Ivy League school Pennsylvania.

"I think it was obvious that the people in Columbus and at Ohio State University in particular were just antsy to get something going in basketball," O'Brien said. "I think *starved* for a little bit more success might be a good way of putting it. You could just tell that there was a lot of interest in trying to get the thing turned around. It didn't take me very long to appreciate the fact that they were patient with me my first year, and it didn't take very long to see the passion that surrounds not only basketball but all the teams, the entire athletic program at Ohio State. The support of the football team is legendary, but when you consider the fact that we had eight wins and we were 1–15 in the conference and we were getting 10,000–11,000 people a game, I thought that was terrific. It could have been a lot worse. I think, coming from the northeast, sometimes it's not always that way. But certainly in Columbus, the people came out and supported us in great fashion, and then the natural thing is, when we became a little bit better, they came out in droves and we enjoyed tremendous fan support."

The Buckeyes were unquestionably bad, having reached rock bottom with their 1–15 showing in conference play during the 1997–98 season. The team was shifting from St. John Arena across the street to the Schottenstein Center. St. John Arena had hosted the team for 42 years and 577 games, drawing more than 6.6 million fans to the venue along the way. Scoonie Penn was becoming eligible following his transfer from Boston College, but he would have to acclimate to playing with new teammates and adapt to sharing the workload with Michael Redd. Many fawned over Redd's sensational freshman season, and for good reason; the standout shooting guard averaged 21.9 points and 6.5 rebounds per game. But O'Brien cautioned that they relied so heavily on Redd to provide offense—and they were so devoid of talent (no one else on the roster averaged more than 10.7 points per game)—that they lowered their standards for him defensively and allowed him to take low-percentage shots on offense since, quite often, little else was available. O'Brien even referred to it as creating a monster, and said that Redd "got away with murder" because they needed "him to score a bundle of points."

"I was basically by myself," Redd said.

Redd was born and raised in Columbus. It pained him to see the Ohio State men's basketball program struggle to such a profound degree in the 1990s. He wanted to stay home and help lift the program out of its slumber, so he committed to the school during those dark days, when the team routinely took up residence in the Big Ten basement.

Penn followed O'Brien to Columbus. The coach marveled at the point guard's competitive spirit, whether he was laying out for a loose ball during a game or emptying his tank to make sure that he won a shooting drill during practice. Penn approached longtime equipment guardian Brice Westfall to request the No. 11 uniform he had worn at Boston College. Penn was confused when he was informed that, even though the school does not officially retire numbers—those special athletes can have their jerseys hang from the rafters, but the numbers are not technically off-limits—the No. 11 was not just handed out to anyone who coveted it. Jerry Lucas, the three-time, consensus first-team All-American and two-time National Player of the Year, wore No. 11. Penn was born 17 years after Lucas was named Most Outstanding Player of the 1960 Final Four, in which Ohio State notched the lone championship in program history.

So, when Penn was told he should choose a different number, he said about Lucas, "Well, he must have been pretty good!" Penn settled on No. 12.

Keels arrived on the scene thinking it would be a long, difficult first year. The program was in transition. O'Brien was welcoming to Keels, but he kept things close to the vest. He was not champing at the bit to participate in interviews and he did not reveal much when he did them, but he understood the responsibilities that Keels had as the team's broadcaster.

But, no, a 27–9 showing and a mad dash to the Final Four was not what anyone had in mind.

It really came out of nowhere.

Redd and Penn spearheaded the offense. Ken Johnson, the behemoth in the post, discouraged opponents from driving to the basket with his penchant for swatting away ill-advised shots. The team also asked more from Redd on the defensive end and with rebounding. Penn emerged as a leader, a natural role for him given that he considered himself a father figure to his younger brother and sister, nephews, niece, and cousins, who all looked up to him. Having a pair of potential stars in the backcourt could have led to some ego-based issues, but both Redd and Penn realized how the other could help their own game. They meshed well on and off the court.

"We really hit it off good the first time we met," Penn said. "I remember the first time I watched him play, I thought, 'This kid is gonna be really good.' I think we had a great relationship ever since that day. We always talk about what we're gonna do, things we want to accomplish in the backcourt."

You would see them play well against the teams they should play well against and you thought, "That's okay, but what are they going to do against the really good teams?" Probably when they won the game at Indiana, where Penn hit some big shots—it had been a long time [eight years] since they won a game at Assembly Hall. When they won the game there, in Bob Knight's next-to-last year coaching there, that really signaled that this team had gotten over a hump, to be able to beat Indiana in Bloomington. That was the one that made you say, "Maybe this team has something special."

The Buckeyes bowed out of the Big Ten Tournament after a 79–77 loss to Illinois in the semifinals at the United Center in Chicago. Ohio State was assigned a No. 4 seed and a date with No. 13 seed Murray

State in Indianapolis in the south region. When No. 5 seed UCLA faltered against No. 12 seed Detroit Mercy in the opening round, that made the path slightly easier. The Buckeyes breezed past the Titans 75–44 to advance to the Sweet 16.

Four teams—the top four seeds in the region—arrived in Knoxville, Tennessee, for the regionals:

- No. 1 Auburn, who started the season 25–1 and stomped its opponents in the SEC.
- No. 2 Maryland, who averaged 85 points per game behind the four-headed monster of Steve Francis, Terence Morris, Laron Profit, and Obinna Ekezie.
- No. 3 St. John's, paced by a balanced scoring attack with five players—including the artist formerly known as Ron Artest—averaging double figures.
- No. 4 Ohio State, who no one expected to reach this stage of the season.

O'Brien made sure his players were not satisfied with a Sweet 16 appearance.

"The thing we talked about throughout the entire tournament was, 'Don't settle,'" he said. "It would be very easy for us to just walk in and say, 'You know, fellas, this has been great, and so if you lose, hey, it's been great. You know, nobody is going to have anything but nice things to say about you. We've achieved more than anyone could have thought we would have.' 'Is this what we want to have? Or do we want to try to get a little bit more? Maybe we can't. But let's see and find out.' I think that's the way they've approached this throughout the entire tournament. 'Let's not be happy with where we are. Let's see if we can get something a little bit more.'"

*The Auburn game was the one you really thought,
"Maybe this is as far as it goes." Chris Porter was a pro-type
player and looked dominant on the court. For them to be able
to get by Auburn, you thought, "This is the most pleasant
surprise of the whole season." They beat a team that had
been highly thought of all year. That made you go,
"Wow. This is a charmed season."*

The Buckeyes knocked out top-seeded Auburn, as Penn and Redd combined to score 48 points. Suddenly, Ohio State fans scrambled to secure tickets and map out the 350-mile trek south on I-71 and I-75 to Thompson-Boling Arena in Knoxville. Few had thought the Buckeyes stood a chance against the kings of the SEC. Buckeyes fans scooped up all of the tickets left behind by disgruntled Auburn and Maryland fans. So many Ohio State fans turned out in Knoxville that the team hotel was clogged to the point that the players and coaches had difficulty getting to their meetings and meals. Ohio State essentially played a home game in Knoxville against St. John's.

*There were a ton of Ohio State fans in the arena for the
St. John's game who were not there the game before.*

The Buckeyes shot 55 percent from the floor to slip past the Red Storm 77–74 and march on to their first Final Four since 1968. Ohio State joined UConn, Duke, and Michigan State as the last teams standing.

*After they clinched the berth of the Final Four, you didn't think
too much about who they were going to play and how it was
going to be. The fact that they had done that a year removed
from losing 20 games was what really blew your mind.*

Ohio State guard Scoonie Penn celebrates his team's fourth-round NCAA Tournament win over St. John's, which earned the Buckeyes their first Final Four appearance since 1968. *Photo courtesy of Getty Images*

Two nights before the semifinal games, the four head coaches—O'Brien, Jim Calhoun, Mike Krzyzewski, and Tom Izzo—gathered together. When Calhoun entered the room, he greeted each of his fellow coaches one by one.

"Tom, it's nice to see you," he said to Izzo.

"Mike, it's nice to see you," he said to Krzyzewski.

"Jim, it's *really* nice to see you," he said to O'Brien.

O'Brien came to Ohio State from Boston College, an old Big East rival of UConn's. He also served as an assistant coach at UConn from 1977 to 1982. O'Brien's teams had lost 18 consecutive games to Calhoun's teams when the coaches clashed again in the Final Four. O'Brien said he believed the Law of Averages would eventually influence the streak of futility, but it never came into play. He thought his players at Boston College had let the shortcomings against UConn develop into a mental hurdle.

"He's probably feeling pretty good that he's playing against me," O'Brien said the day before the game. "Maybe not so much against our team, but hopefully we'll be able to get a little bit lucky and end some of what has gone on in the past."

The Buckeyes entered as a confident bunch. At media day, Redd spoke about his improved defense, his top focus throughout the season (his scoring average dropped a bit in the process). O'Brien praised Penn when talking about the four teams' talented point guards, with Michigan State's Mateen Cleaves, Duke's William Avery, and UConn's Khalid El-Amin also receiving plaudits.

Duke garnered most of the national attention, and for good reason. They blitzed through their ACC schedule, with an unblemished 16–0 mark. Their only loss of the season had come against Cincinnati, by two points, on the third night of a back-to-back-to-back in the Great Alaska Shootout at Sullivan Arena in Anchorage in late November. The Blue Devils entered the Final Four riding a 31-game winning streak, and they were captained by big man Elton Brand, the National Player of the Year. The Buckeyes happily played into that narrative, too.

"I feel like we're playing an undercard," Penn said. "We probably don't get spoken about as much as the other teams. [Duke is] the No. 1 seed. We're the No. 4 seed. But I feel like that's okay with us. I feel like we've been in that situation all season, kind of playing the underdog role. It fit us well, so we'll continue playing it."

The game was billed as a battle of brilliant backcourts, with Penn and Redd opposing El-Amin and Richard Hamilton. Redd boasted that no one could halt Ohio State's dynamic duo. El-Amin said UConn's two-some "felt threatened that they were going to try to outdo us."

Ohio State ran out of steam in the national semifinal meeting with UConn, the eventual champion. The Huskies finished the season with a 34–2 record, and they held the Buckeyes to 37 percent shooting, including a 10-for-31 effort from Penn and Redd, at Tropicana Field in St. Petersburg, Florida. UConn's vaunted defense lived up to the hype. Ricky Moore, who Penn described as "one of the best on-the-ball defensive players in the country," was tasked with slowing down Ohio State's point guard.

"He's going to give us problems," Penn said, in prophetic fashion.

Moore did just that.

"Scoonie Penn is one of the best players we have ever gone against," said Huskies coach Jim Calhoun. "He was 3-for-13....I think Scoonie Penn is going to be—I don't want to say the next level, because there are not many better levels than this, but [he will play] professional basketball. He's going to make a lot of money playing basketball. Basically, [Moore] cut the head of the dragon off. Scoonie, to me, is all about what happens. If Scoonie goes, so does Ohio State."

Might it have been the clothes that made the man struggle? Penn's scarlet No. 12 uniform was nowhere to be found in the locker room before the game, so he instead played in a nameless No. 35 jersey, known as the "blood jersey," since it was saved for if someone needed a mid-game replacement because of a blood spill.

"He just didn't let me breathe," Penn said. "The whole time. He did a great job on defense."

UConn topped Duke in the title game two days later, 77–74, in a heavyweight battle.

Both Penn and Redd said they had no reason to hang their heads. The program had reversed course, from 8–22 to 27–9 and a spot in the Final Four. After the game, O'Brien told his players in the locker room to concentrate on the big picture and the year-over-year progress, not the single loss in St. Petersburg, despite the disappointment that accompanied it.

"When you get to this point, you never know when you're going to get an opportunity to get back into this Final Four setting," O'Brien said. "And when you think in terms of being one game away from playing for the national championship, it's almost a surreal expression to me, so that's the disappointing thing, [that] you get this far and you're not able to get the whole thing. But absolutely nothing is going to happen to take away the feeling that I have of accomplishment and the feeling of appreciation for what our kids did this year. So this really hurts, but I think back on how this whole thing has gone, and it's not going to be that bad after we get out of here and we start thinking about when we first started practice back in September, with all of the learning. This is not that big of a deal to me right now. The big picture is so much more important.

"I'm hoping that in some small way, we've been able to restore some of the respectability to Ohio State's basketball program, and if that's the case, then maybe some of the younger players in the state of Ohio would take a little closer look at our program at this point. Because, obviously, that's going to continue to be the life of the program. So hopefully we've been able to restore some of the dignity that I think the university deserves."

Penn said O'Brien was responsible for changing the culture, making the players believe in the program and instilling a winning attitude, despite the team's recent track record.

The fact that that team got to the Final Four, having lost 20 games the year before, it was truly, truly amazing. Ohio State basketball, when going well, can really excite people. While the season ended with a defeat, there was new enthusiasm for Ohio State basketball.

CHAPTER 3
A NATIONAL
CHAMPIONSHIP
NO ONE SAW COMING

Consider Paul Keels' first four years in the Ohio State football radio booth:

- 1998: No. 1 team for much of the season, loses November game to unranked Michigan State
- 1999: Unranked team, doesn't go to a bowl game for the first time in a decade
- 2000: 8–4 team, John Cooper dismissed at the end of the season
- 2001: Jim Tressel's first year, team ends up 7–5

What would the 2002 campaign have in store? Oh, just a historic 14–0 record and an exhilarating and often agonizing march to a national championship in an all-time classic of a title game that was dangerous for the health of any fan with an investment in the outcome.

The foundation was placed a year earlier, when Tressel came aboard and immediately promised the Buckeyes would put forth a valiant effort against rival Michigan. Tressel grabbed a microphone during halftime of Ohio State's 78–61 win against Michigan in basketball on January 18, 2001, and declared to the crowd, "You'll be proud of our young people in the classroom, in the community and, most especially, in 310 days in Ann Arbor, Michigan, on the football field." The fans in attendance at the Schottenstein Center erupted toward the end of that sentence.

After the fact, it always seemed like you'd run into people who would say he predicted that Ohio State would beat Michigan. Well, no, that wasn't quite what he said.

Things were a bit different with Tressel now patrolling the sideline in place of John Cooper. Practices that previously had been open to a select few were no longer open. Player availability had diminished, especially after Ohio State lost a game, though that did not happen too frequently after Tressel's first year at the helm. The access that media members had to the team decreased significantly.

Tressel earned the nickname "the Senator" for a reason. He was polished and eloquent and had a knack for saying a lot of words that amounted to very little substance. To this day, Keels occasionally runs into basketball coaches who spent time working in Ohio and who joke, "Oh, yeah, I remember listening to the weekly radio show you used to do with Tressel. No matter who they were playing, it all sounded the same. You could just substitute the opponent."

Tressel was all about respecting the opponent, no matter the team's record or talent level. Tressel was all about playing the game the right way, with a steady rushing attack, a quality defense, and most importantly, a fundamentally sound special teams unit. You want to feel the sort of pressure that tenses up your shoulder muscles and creates beads of sweat on your forearms and on the back of your neck? Try being a punter on one of Tressel's teams.

Tressel was all about his senior players. He insisted that, on each weekly radio show episode, the network would have at least one senior player on for a segment. Sometimes, it would be a walk-on player who did not even appear in the media guide, which made it difficult for Keels to find the proper questions to ask.

You would get a few of them who were great at doing the interviews, and some of them would freeze up and be nervous as all hell. It was very different with Tressel. Once we got a routine going with him, he was very consistent for all of the stuff we had to bother him with. It became routine. But it was very, very different.

Ohio State was supposed to host San Diego State on September 15, 2001, but the tragic events of September 11 forced the teams to modify their schedules. So San Diego State traveled east for an October 20 matchup at the Horseshoe instead. Craig Krenzel missed that game to attend his sister's wedding, initially scheduled for an Ohio State bye week.

Krenzel consulted Tressel and the team's assistant coaches. The Buckeyes had four quarterbacks on the roster, and Krenzel had not appeared in a game by that point in the season. Krenzel missed the game, but he would soon factor into the team's plans under center.

Krenzel and Scott McMullen replaced Steve Bellisari after the starter was slapped with a one-game suspension because of a drunk driving arrest. Ohio State lost to Illinois in its first game with Krenzel and McMullen at the helm. Tressel reinstated Bellisari for the Michigan game, but listed the senior as the team's No. 4 quarterback. Krenzel—a native of Utica, Michigan—got the start, and he guided the Buckeyes to victory in Ann Arbor, 310 days after Tressel was introduced as head coach.

After they beat Michigan up there, it had everybody wondering what could happen the next year.

Krenzel played only the first series in Ohio State's bowl game, another loss to South Carolina in the Outback Bowl. Bellisari relieved him and accounted for three touchdowns in the 31–28 defeat.

"There were ups and downs that year," Tressel said.

But the table had been set. Krenzel would lead the team the following season. Award-winning safety Mike Doss decided to return for his senior year. Tressel had a year of experience at the controls in Columbus and familiarity with his players. Things were looking up. Not necessarily "undefeated and talented enough to slay the invincible college football dragon" up, but the Buckeyes seemed poised to improve on their 7–5 mark from Tressel's first year at the helm.

Everybody thought it would be the following year (2003) when they would really contend.

Ohio State began the 2002 season ranked No. 13 in the country. Two of their first three games came against Heisman Trophy–hopeful quarterbacks, in Texas Tech's Kliff Kingsbury and No. 10 Washington State's Jason Gesser. The Buckeyes had no trouble with either opponent, and they carried a 3–0 record into their first road game of the season, a date with Cincinnati at Paul Brown Stadium. It marked Ohio State's first road game against an Ohio team within the state since they demolished Case Western Reserve 76–0, in November 1934. It was the Buckeyes' first trip to Cincinnati in 91 years.

That game ended up being a sign of what the games were going to be all season: nail-biters.

The Reds were playing their final series at Cinergy Field before they relocated to Great American Ball Park. The Friday night game against the Phillies was rained out, so the Reds hosted a doubleheader at their venue on Saturday. It was also Oktoberfest weekend in the downtown area. And Ohio State and Cincinnati had a 3:35 PM kickoff. It was a chaotic weekend in the Queen City, and it was especially meaningful for Keels, a Cincinnati native and former Cincinnati broadcaster. He had plenty of friends in attendance at the football game.

When Ohio State fired John Cooper after the 2000 season, Rick Minter, the head coach at Cincinnati placed a call to Keels to gauge the situation. The two had gotten to know each other well when Keels was calling Bearcats games, before he moved north to Columbus. Minter picked Keels' brain about the program's direction, which coaching candidates they had interest in, whether they would even consider him if he expressed intrigue in the opening. The university ended up tabbing Tressel as its top coach, but Minter and the Bearcats gave the Buckeyes all they could handle when the two sides clashed in Cincinnati in 2002.

A pair of fourth-quarter interceptions saved the Buckeyes' season from plummeting to the ground before it ever really took off. A two-way player was born that afternoon in Cincinnati. Chris Gamble, a sophomore receiver, entered on defense for the first time and intercepted

Bearcats quarterback Gino Guidugli in the end zone with 11 minutes remaining. Gamble would wind up earning a sizable chunk of playing time both at receiver and at cornerback, exhibiting a rare level of endurance and athleticism. Will Allen sealed the 23–19 victory with an interception in that same end zone with 26 seconds remaining.

After the game, Minter stressed that there "was no solace in playing them close. We had a chance to win the ballgame and we didn't take it."

"I don't think we were at the top of our game from a focus standpoint," Tressel said. "Sometimes when you look in the mirror, you say to yourself, 'I don't know why I allowed myself to not be as good as I could be today.' We need to evaluate ourselves individually and learn a lesson. It's interesting how we have to repeat the learning of lessons. I would like to think we could learn a lesson once and for all, but sometimes we do not. I think that we learned when you play against a good football team like Cincinnati without 100 percent focus, then it will be an interesting day. I'm not sure we had our best preparation week and we did not have our best execution. What was most telling about Saturday was that we did not have our best decision-making day."

It seemed like most every week it was, "How are they going to find a different way to hang on and win a football game?"

There was the 19–14 win at Wisconsin. Krenzel tossed a three-yard touchdown pass to tight end Ben Hartsock to complete an 88-yard drive in the fourth quarter that fueled Ohio State's narrow victory. Freshman running back Maurice Clarett carried the ball 30 times for 133 yards.

"I was catching that with every part of my body possible," Hartsock said after the game. "It was like there was a baby in there."

There was the 13–7 win against Penn State, a victory attainable only because Gamble returned an interception for a touchdown. After the score, Keels and broadcast partner Jim Lachey both removed their headphones to hear the roar from the crazed crowd.

*We can't really hear the crowd like everybody else does
with our headphones and our microphones on. I remember
when we did that, how ungodly loud that stadium was.
It just bowled you over.*

Penn State quarterback Zack Mills said he made "a terrible pass. I may have tried to force some things. We had one good drive and that was it." Coach Joe Paterno was impressed by Ohio State, but not blown away by the Buckeyes.

"I think they are the best team we faced this year," he said. "It would be between them and Iowa."

Nittany Lions receiver Tony Johnson—the son of future Ohio State defensive line coach Larry Johnson Sr.—took it a step further. "They have a lot more athletes than Iowa," he said, "but better? No."

Even in late October, there was plenty of skepticism about Ohio State's credentials. During Tressel's weekly press luncheon, a few days before the Penn State game, he was asked about the team carrying an unbeaten record into the final month of the regular season.

"We have only played eight games," he said. "That is little more than half the year. They asked me on the Big Ten media call: would we be outraged if we [win out and are not included in the BCS title game]? Football is not something to get outraged about. I would be outraged if we don't play well on Saturday, maybe more than if we don't win every game."

They kept playing well enough to win—even if sometimes it was *barely* well enough to win—and they preserved their undefeated standing into November.

"In the end," Doss said, "whatever the BCS says, that's what it says."

There was the 10–6 win at Purdue, the "pull a rabbit with gold-speckled fur out of your hat" variety of victory. It was a gloomy, Saturday afternoon on a muddy field, conditions that contributed to a lackluster Buckeyes offense.

That was the one that you thought, "Ehhh, maybe this is where it runs out. This might be the end of it here."

Tell that to Krenzel and his always reliable receiver Michael Jenkins. The two connected for a miracle of a touchdown on fourth-and-1 in the waning moments of the fourth quarter. The play that became known as "Holy Buckeye" in Columbus rescued the Buckeyes from the jaws of defeat and a disconcerting way to bow out of the national championship race.

"It's a situation I wish everybody in the world could feel," Krenzel said, "with that kind of excitement, that natural high."

Later that day, as the Buckeyes were waiting to take off on their flight for Columbus, they were watching No. 1 Oklahoma's matchup against Texas A&M at Kyle Field in College Station, Texas. The Aggies pulled off the upset by a 30–26 score, and that left Ohio State and Miami as the only unbeaten teams remaining in college football.

That's when you think, "Maybe now the deck has been cleared for them to get to that BCS Championship Game." That part gets to be fun, especially when it's over and you can ruminate on it a little bit.

Ohio State jumped to No. 2 in the nation after that weekend's action, but the task didn't get any simpler.

"We're not going to drop in the Big Ten standings," Tressel said after the win in West Lafayette, Indiana, "and that is what's important right now."

That year, we paid a lot of attention to what was going on with the other schools that were unbeaten. You heard all of the prognosticators say, "Well, if there are more than two unbeaten teams, because of the way Ohio State was playing,

would they be included?" You could understand why some
people were saying, "Well, maybe not."

There was the 23–16 overtime win at Illinois. In the days leading up to the game, the Big Ten public relations staff mentioned in their game notes that Ohio State was the only team in the conference that had not played in an overtime game since the overtime rules were instituted. Naturally, the Buckeyes needed an extra period to put away the pesky Fighting Illini.

In our job, you watch the game differently than you do as a
fan. You don't have the same ups and downs and the rising
blood pressure and things like that. But it is fun, because,
especially with a team like that, it's like, "Who is going to
make the next play? When is Clarett all of a sudden going to
tear off a big run? When is Krenzel going to slip away and
make a conversion?" Chris Gamble was the headliner playing
on both sides of the ball. When is he going to make a big play?
The defensive line and those linebackers—really, that whole
defense, with Mike Doss and Donnie Nickey and Dustin Fox.
You just waited. Even if they were playing lousy, like they did
at Purdue, you thought, "Who is going to do something to turn
this around? Will the magic continue?" It was a lot of fun. You
wanted to see if they could really keep continuing to do this.

There was the 14–9 clincher against Michigan, the sort of game in which Ohio State notched its two touchdowns and then held on for dear life. Not until Allen clutched the football in his hands and went down to the ground after a last-second interception of Wolverines quarterback John Navarre could Ohio State fans breathe comfortably. After all, they had witnessed so many examples of Michigan dismantling an otherwise perfectly constructed Ohio State season.

Ohio State free safety Will Allen (26) is mobbed by teammates after picking off a pass near the goal line on the game's final play, as the Buckeyes beat Michigan at home, 14–9, on November 23, 2002, to remain undefeated.

Michigan had ruined so many of their chances against Cooper's teams.

The Wolverines had rejected the Buckeyes' bids for unbeaten seasons in both 1995 and 1996. So six days before the 2002 game, Earle Bruce spoke to the team to preach the importance of the rivalry, the stakes, and the legacy that the group could create for itself.

"We are feeding off the pressure," said senior safety Donnie Nickey. "Everything is on the line: if we win, we go [to the Fiesta Bowl to play for the national championship], and if we don't win, we don't go. We are feeding off that. We know what we have to do."

Krenzel stood at the epicenter of the hype machine. He opted to attend Ohio State over Michigan because he desired to move away from home, rather than enroll in a school that sat about 45 minutes from his family's residence. It was a year earlier when Krenzel commanded the offense and offered a preview of how Ohio State could fare the following season, with Bellisari having exhausted his eligibility. Now, he had a chance to bring everything full circle.

Matt Wilhelm had to decide between Ohio State and Michigan, as well. The linebacker sat in the stands on a recruiting visit for the 1998 battle between the two rivals. He treasured the atmosphere at Ohio Stadium and how the fans rushed onto the field following the Buckeyes' 31–16 triumph against the Wolverines on that Saturday afternoon.

Doss actually wanted to attend Michigan at first. His decision ultimately boiled down to Michigan, Ohio State, and Penn State. With some influence from his family, the Canton, Ohio, native opted to stay close to home.

When Bruce imparted his wisdom upon the team, he stressed the significance of protecting the football. He cautioned that, in any Ohio State–Michigan game, turnovers can sink even the most talented bunch. Sure enough, the Buckeyes did not commit a turnover, and Allen's interception sealed the victory, which immediately resulted in tears streaming down Doss' face. He hustled to midfield and began to pray. His decision to return for his senior season had been validated.

"In the four years Mike has played here and the five years that I have been here," Nickey said after the game, "[the seniors] have been though all the stuff and we have seen it all. When Will caught the ball, there were no words for it."

And on to Tempe, Arizona, it was. It was not always pretty—in fact, it was often pretty unsightly—but the Buckeyes punched their ticket to the Fiesta Bowl to play for the national title.

"We might not go out and score 50 points. We might not hold teams to 10 yards," said Maurice Clarett, who accounted for the first of Ohio State's two touchdowns. "But we make the plays when we have to."

Maurice Hall handed Ohio State the lead with just under five minutes remaining on a three-yard touchdown scamper. Michigan committed a pair of turnovers in the game's final 122 seconds, including Allen's grab as the clock flashed all zeroes. Buckeyes defensive coordinator (and future Michigan State head coach) Mark Dantonio referred to the safety as the team's "miracle man."

"We have a scrappy, tough, talented, smart bunch of folks who want to achieve," Tressel said.

Said athletic director Andy Geiger, "I did not think that we could run the table, especially with the 13-game season. They kept at it all season. This is an incredibly hard-working team."

Keels thinks back to his first season on the job in 1998 and the sky-high expectations attached to Ohio State. Then he reflects upon the 1999 team, which sat at home in December and on New Year's Day as other teams battled in their bowl games. He laughs.

All of a sudden, 2002, who really would have expected it at the start? And then, even as the year went on, with all of the nail-biters, could they keep everything going to get into the BCS Championship Game?

It seemingly became more and more challenging, but Tressel's crew kept unearthing new ways to sidestep defeat. And for their troubles, they were rewarded with a date with a Miami team that had not suffered a loss in 846 days. The Hurricanes had assembled a 34-game winning streak, which made Ohio State's 13-game win streak seem rather pedestrian.

Once the Buckeyes dispatched Michigan and earned their title game berth, they still had to wait two weeks to see if Miami would be the team to meet them in Arizona in early January. The Hurricanes trounced

Syracuse and beat No. 18 Virginia Tech to secure their spot. In the end, Ohio State had six weeks off before the championship duel.

I think that's what led people to think that the Ohio State team didn't have much of a chance against Miami. It was such a long period of time. There was no conference championship game.

Perhaps people underestimated the Ohio State defense. Over the final seven games of the regular season, the Buckeyes limited the opposition to 7.8 points per contest. The unit was flooded with future NFL players, from defensive end Will Smith—a first-round selection by the New Orleans Saints in 2004—to Gamble, the Carolina Panthers' first-round choice in 2004.

In fact, there was a litany of talent on both sides of the ball for both teams in the national title game. Of the 43 starters in the glorified all-star game, 37 of them ultimately became NFL draft picks. Smith, Gamble, Jenkins, center Nick Mangold, and linebackers A.J. Hawk and Bobby Carpenter proceeded to be first-round selections. Even some backups, who saw the field sparingly during the double-overtime thriller, reached the professional ranks. Of the 100 players who appeared in the game, 58 participated in at least one NFL contest.

As it was going on, you realized you were seeing a collection of very special athletes out there.

It felt like a home game for Ohio State. The stands were a sea of scarlet. The crowd seemed to roar when the Buckeyes soared and groan when they sputtered.

Once you got into the stadium and the fans started coming in, that's the first thing that jumped out at you was how the Ohio State fans outnumbered the Miami fans.

Keels' first in-game observation was that Miami quarterback Ken Dorsey looked like he was not accustomed to being hurried and knocked to the grass. Smith forced the signal-caller to the ground on the Hurricanes' first play from scrimmage. The Silver Bullets made that a routine occurrence.

You could tell that offensive line and Dorsey had not been harassed like that. That made you think. They were having no trouble with anybody all season long. Those first few plays made you think Ohio State could make a game out of it.

Miami entered the affair as a 13-point favorite, though that did not prevent Dorsey from saying, a few days before the game, "We're favorites? Could have fooled me." Yeah, the team riding the nearly three-season-long winning streak was considered the favorite against a scrappy bunch that barely escaped defeat against middling Big Ten opponents.

During a media session, Dantonio was asked about the challenges Miami's offense presented. The defensive coordinator said it would be "a great challenge for us. We look forward to that. The thing I have experienced since being here is we play with great confidence. We're very competitive."

He then looked over to Doss, sitting beside him and asked: "Are you afraid?"

"Not at all," Doss said.

Still, there was a clear-cut narrative that Miami was Goliath and Ohio State was David. In fact, during a press conference earlier in the week, one reporter asked defensive lineman Kenny Peterson if he was confident Ohio State was going to win the game. What was he supposed to say, no?

"Of course," Peterson said. "You don't want to go into a fight saying, 'I'm going to lose.' Of course you have confidence going into any game, no matter [if you are] playing PlayStation or football. I'm confident in our offense and defense. We are putting together a pretty good scheme. We have to go out and see what happens."

A couple of minutes later, a different reporter asked Wilhelm, sitting beside Peterson, about the volume of media attention at the Fiesta Bowl.

Reporter: "What's the silliest thing you have been asked about?"

Wilhelm: "The question she just asked."

Peterson: "Right. That was the weirdest thing."

Wilhelm: "Do we feel confident we're going to win? I think if any of us were not confident, we would have never gotten on a plane to come to Tempe."

All week, Ohio State players were bombarded with questions about Miami's team speed and athletic prowess. The Buckeyes did not mind being underdogs, but the national narrative was readily apparent.

"You don't go, 'Wow,'" Clarett said. "Everybody puts their pants on the same way. Anything can happen."

Darrion Scott was asked to speak about Miami being "loaded offensively" and "scary to watch."

"They're impressive," Scott said, "but like any other team, they can be stopped. That's why you have game plans and whatnot. You make game plans to stop a team. You put in different defenses or blitzes to prevent the quarterback and not give him time to pick you apart. They're a great team and have great weapons. We also have a great defense."

Then Scott was asked if he would go into the game confident about opposing Miami. Again, what was he supposed to say, that he thinks Miami will win by four touchdowns? No one seemed to be giving the Buckeyes a chance, but Tressel said the coaching staff never mentioned the word underdog in preparation for the game.

"We're going to go into this game confident," Scott said. "I can't see why we would go into this game not being confident. I think we can come out victorious."

For Keels and Lachey, it was business as usual. They tried to prepare as if it were any other game. It helped that Miami played twice after Ohio State's regular season came to an end, so they gained some extra familiarity with the Hurricanes' roster and storylines. Plus, Miami was always on TV, always on during prime time, so they had already established a base of knowledge about the Buckeyes' opponent. Keels had grown accustomed to calling University of Cincinnati games earlier in his career. The thought of broadcasting a national championship game would have seemed foreign to him during his tenure with the Bearcats. He did his best not to get caught up in the moment and the hype. One of the employees on the radio station's pregame show asked Keels if he had a line prepared for the end of the game if Ohio State were to win the championship.

I was like, "No, I usually thought if you tried to rehearse something like that, it would probably end up coming off sounding like it was rehearsed and phony and canned."

Once the game started, the job became routine in the broadcast booth. Mention the score, the down, and the yardage every so often. Properly identify the players involved in the action. Describe what is unfolding on the field.

That became imperative when a controversial pass-interference call awarded the Buckeyes an extra life in overtime. On fourth-and-3 from the 5-yard line, the Buckeyes' last gasp, needing a touchdown to force a second extra period, Miami defensive back Glenn Sharpe was whistled for interference on Gamble in the end zone. Field judge Terry Porter said he watched Sharpe hold Gamble prior to Krenzel throwing the ball in their direction and that Sharpe was still holding him and pulling him down once the football was in flight. He certainly took his sweet time to yank the yellow flag from his side and heave it to the grass.

"He was holding me," Gamble said. "He was in my face mask and my shoulder pads. I was waiting for the flag, but he kind of hesitated. I didn't see him going for the flag and I thought, 'He ain't going to throw it.' Luckily, he did, and I'm like, 'Whew.'"

We started saying, "The dream season has come to an end."

Miami players had rolled their helmets onto the field. Krenzel had been knocked to the ground and he stayed there, helmet in hand.

"To be honest," Krenzel said, "it was a feeling of dejection, thinking the game was over, knowing how hard we played and how much effort we put in, and just at that time thinking we weren't victorious. I thought there was contact, but I didn't see the flag until after I got up. I think it was the right call."

They started to celebrate on the Hurricanes' sideline. The officials attempted to calm everybody down. Meanwhile, in the broadcast booth, Lachey noticed the penalty flag.

Jim is yelling on air at the top of his lungs about 12 times.

"There's a flag! There's a flag! There's a flag!"

*Even his relatives still give him grief about how loud he was
yelling it. When that happened, all of a sudden, it was like,
'Well, here's this team that finds another way to stay alive.'
They were able to find a way to keep that drive going and get
in the end zone and score.*

In Keels' home office, a picture hangs on the wall of the final play from that game, with the Ohio State defense lined up and the Miami offense in formation, the Hurricanes needing to reach the end zone on fourth-and-goal, a few inches from the 1-yard line in double overtime.

---

*That was one of those where you could feel the way the
momentum had swung, and you liked Ohio State's chances of
stopping them on that last play.*

In the huddle, Doss told his teammates, "Somebody has to make a play. Let everyone step up. This is the last play in the world."

And then Brett Romberg snapped the ball to Dorsey.

Cie Grant rushed freely from the edge and hurried Dorsey back toward the 13-yard line and forced him into an undesirable throw, not to one of his many weapons such as Andre Johnson or Roscoe Parrish or Kellen Winslow, but to the center of the field, just in front of the end zone, where only a group of Ohio State defenders stood, so the football plunged, harmlessly, to the grass, away from the grasp of any Miami receiver and the tens of thousands of fans clad in scarlet in the stands erupted, bouncing up and down and shrieking until their voice boxes tapped out for the night.

Exhale.

The Buckeyes did it. Somehow, some way.

We were all in our radio booth, sitting there and looking at each other like, "Can you believe this team just won a national championship? Did they really do that?"

Keels and Lachey spent about an hour and a half on the air following the final whistle, as Tressel hoisted the Crystal Football and Ohio State players and coaches donned championship shirts and hats and held newspapers with headlines in 72-point type. Krenzel missed the bus that drove the players back to the team hotel because he spent so much time doing interviews and posing for pictures and talking to his family. He instead traveled back to the hotel in one of the officer's cars from the team's police escort.

The final question in the postgame press conference was posed to Doss about the magnitude of what the team had accomplished, slaying the dragon on the grand stage in an epic, back-and-forth battle to place the final chapter on an incredible script of an action-packed season.

"It's still unbelievable to hear those fireworks go off and to rush the field," Doss said. "We won the game, but it was the game on the national

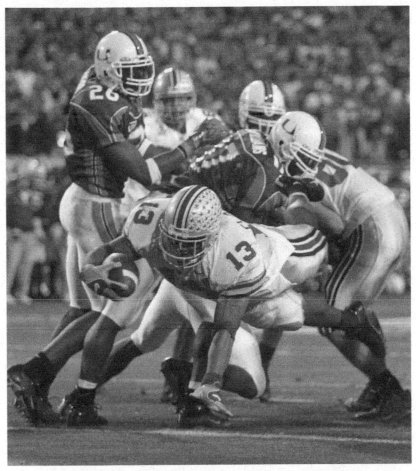

Ohio State tailback Maurice Clarett (13) dives into the end zone against Miami for a five-yard touchdown in the second overtime of the BCS Championship Game at the Fiesta Bowl in Tempe, Arizona, on January 3, 2003.

stage, two overtimes. We're sitting here, looking at each other. We're little kids in the candy store. It's Christmas for us."

At that time, Tressel pointed out Rex Kern, the quarterback who guided Ohio State to its previous national championship in 1968.

"I want to congratulate you and your team," Kern said, "the way that you won and doing what you guys set out to do. We're proud of the football team and our coach and what you've accomplished. And timetables, they always want to tie you down. I would give a comment of what Woody would say, but I won't. Congratulations."

Keels had a morning flight back to Columbus the next day. He, Lachey, and the rest of the broadcast team retreated to the team hotel, where they were staying. One of the guys in the group had been assigned a spacious, two-room suite, equipped with a vast living room and dining room and a kitchen area, because the hotel screwed up his reservation. So, in the days leading up to the game, the radio crew had filled that room with coolers of beer and pop and ice and snacks. The group returned to that suite after the game, and the guy invited a couple of his college buddies to join them. They cracked open some beers, smoked some cigars, and reflected on what they had all just witnessed. As word spread around the hotel that all bars and restaurants in the area had closed, more and more people started to show up to the suite. Soon, the place turned into party central. At one point, Keels turned around and noticed former Cleveland Indians pitcher Charles Nagy in the same room. Ohio State employees and members of the athletic department arrived. There was nowhere else to celebrate, nowhere else to try to wrap their heads around the instant classic they had just watched.

There was still the same disbelief that this team had done what it had done.

After a couple of hours of sleep, Keels and his comrades boarded the plane to return to Columbus. Ohio State had a basketball game the next day against Louisville at the Schottenstein Center, but Keels had the day off, since he was traveling. He needed the breather. So did many others.

You could sense relief for a team that had made so many close calls. They finally got through the final close call that year.

WHAT OHIO STADIUM MEANS TO ME

by Paul Keels

For many of us, it is a stretch to envision the Buckeyes playing any-where but Ohio Stadium. To read about and hear the stories of fans cramming old Ohio Field to watch Chic Harley's exploits tells you quite a bit about how far back the fever raged for Ohio State football. Harley helped to lay the groundwork for what ultimately evolved into a glob-ally renowned program. He chose to attend Ohio State instead of Notre Dame, Michigan, or Army, and the university changed forever.

Harley ran the ball, passed the ball, caught the ball, intercepted the ball, and even kicked the ball for the Buckeyes. He steered Ohio State to its first Big Ten championship with an undefeated season in 1916. He was named a consensus first-team All-American and attracted national attention to the program. A surge in attendance fol-lowed, which triggered the idea for a new football stadium. Ohio Field could not meet the new demands of the fan base. The Buckeyes went unbeaten again in 1917.

Despite various changes through the years at the Horseshoe, the building still holds much of the character that can link fans to the past. While the wizardry of the scoreboard and video screen can cap-ture people's attention, you can still look at the sidelines and imagine Woody Hayes pleading with the officials as only he could. A crushing blow by Jack Tatum, a slippery escape by Eddie George, a dart thrown by Bobby Hoying, and the galloping of Howard "Hopalong" Cassidy—those moments all took place on the same field upon which today's Buckeyes perform.

Ohio Stadium is not only the cathedral of Ohio State football, but in recent years it has hosted high school stars who have claimed state titles, as the prep championships have returned to central Ohio. The Ohio State men's lacrosse team has performed on the sacred ground. Weddings and private events have been staged at the same location where Jim Stillwagon and his teammates knocked off No. 1 Purdue in 1968. Even the Rolling Stones and the Buckeye Country Superfest have lured music lovers to the grounds where Big Ten titles have been decided.

The legendary stadium can mean so much to so many people. It is where they attended games with their parents and children. It is where they celebrated birthdays and anniversaries. It is where they watched unforgettable triumphs and heartbreaking defeats. And for some, the most memorable occasions might have taken place outside of the massive structure. Tailgate parties have become works of art themselves. Some people even use the spring game as a practice run for how their season tailgate routine will operate.

Here are some memories from 20 years worth of fall Saturdays spent at the venue:

- During the cherished championship season of 2002—one filled with close calls and thrilling finishes—our radio crew began holding impromptu postgame get-togethers in our stadium parking lot area. As the record-setting season unfolded, friends and relatives would join our gatherings, especially those who lived nearby and did not attend the game. As seasons went on, the tailgate gathering started growing larger. Ultimately, some university staffers would join the fun. There was even an instance in which Ohio State president E. Gordon Gee made a quick fly-by to wish us all well.

- The 2007 season opener was memorable at Ohio Stadium, though not so much for the Buckeyes' Week 1 win against Jim Tressel's old Youngstown State program. Instead, it was all about what was happening in Ann Arbor, Michigan, on the same afternoon. As we were conducting our lengthy postgame show from the radio booth, it seemed there was some sort of ruckus occurring in the concourse areas out of our sight lines. Fans had gathered around some of the TV screens near concession stands to watch the final minutes of Michigan's opener against Appalachian State, and the Wolverines were in a struggle with the Mountaineers, who at the time were in the Football Championship Subdivision level (what many used to know as Division I-AA).

As Michigan was staging a final drive with little time remaining, the people at Ohio Stadium put the telecast on the giant video board in the south end of the stadium so that those remaining in the stands, and even people in the parking lots with the scoreboard in their view, could watch the game's conclusion. Sure enough, Appalachian State blocked a potential game-winning field-goal attempt and scored the historic upset. It marked the first time an FCS school had defeated a ranked FBS program. The roar from the Buckeyes fans in and around the stadium that day might have rivaled any of theirs from the game played between Ohio State and Youngstown State.

The following summer, I attended the annual National Association of Sportscasters and Sportswriters Awards weekend in Salisbury, North Carolina. At the first event of the trip, I was hastily approached by a gentleman who was a sportswriter for the local newspaper in Salisbury. He had heard the story about the reaction of Ohio State fans to the monumental upset staged by the Boone, North Carolina, school and he was seeking quotes from someone who was there to experience it. A memorable time in the stadium lived on hundreds of miles away (and several months later).

• One particular Saturday in November, following the final home game of the season, a group of us gathered together in the parking lot for our final tailgate of the year. While it was dark, one of our tailgaters noticed the people who were working inside the stadium were disposing of leftover items from the private suites, including several bunches of bananas. The person approached the stadium employee and saved the bananas. The end result: bananas dipped in the vanilla cognac that was part of our tailgate supply, which made for quite a dessert to end the home season.

- A number of summers ago, I was able to arrange a stadium tour for some Ohio State fans I know who split their time between Ohio and Florida. They were able to see the press box and the locker rooms and walk on the field. The parents in this group were especially thrilled to experience the band facilities within the stadium. Their daughter got more of a kick out of visiting the bell tower in the southeast corner of Ohio Stadium and ringing the victory bell.

Ohio Stadium filled to capacity for a game in September 2017.

- On a gameday at Ohio Stadium, the sight of people taking pictures at the rotunda at the north end of the stadium never grows old. You can see the ROTC groups drilling around the stadium grounds, detect the smells of all of the food being grilled, spot the countless flags raised from the ends of vehicles in the surrounding parking lots, and hear the band parading to St. John Arena for the pregame Skull Session.
- The vantage point we enjoy from the radio booth in the press box is never taken for granted. We are positioned at midfield and are high above all of the seating areas. It provides a helpful view for pregame field-level prep. The insides come to life when the gates open and the fans enter and eagerly await the home team's march from the north end toward the locker rooms in the southeast part of the stadium. We get to watch the visiting team's entrance and can observe, in many cases, their tourist-like approach to a new building.

  Then comes perhaps one of the most exciting things that occurs in the stadium, prior to kickoff: the Ohio State Marching Band's entrance from the north tunnel. The thunderous applause that greets these master musicians often equals the magical sounds that emit from their instruments. It is always a great recommendation for someone attending a game at Ohio Stadium for the first time to make sure they are in their seat before the band's arrival. Then the sight of the band performing Script Ohio and the dotting of the i is always memorable, no matter how many times you see it.

CHAPTER 4
THE THAD FIVE

The tide had definitely shifted. Ohio State's men's basketball program had risen from conference cellar-dweller to perennial NCAA Tournament participant. But the team could never recreate the magic of that 1999 Final Four run under Jim O'Brien. And worse, there was a program-shaking scandal brewing beneath the surface.

The following three seasons, the Buckeyes were left disappointed in March, dismissed by a lower seed in the tournament.

2000
Seed: 3
Overall: 23–7 (13–3 in Big Ten)
Tournament result: 75–62 loss to No. 6 seed Miami in 2nd round

2001
Seed: 5
Overall: 20–11 (11–5 in Big Ten)
Tournament result: 77–68 loss to No. 12 seed Utah State in 1st round

2002
Seed: 4
Overall: 24–8 (11–5 in Big Ten)
Tournament result: 83–67 loss to No. 12 seed Missouri in 2nd round

The next two seasons, Ohio State missed the tournament altogether. The Buckeyes combined to register a 31–31 record, including a 13–19 showing in conference play. They surrendered more points than they scored. In 2003 they lost to Georgia Tech in the first round of the NIT. The following year, they took an early spring break. A first-round defeat in the Big Ten Tournament in Indianapolis marked their final game of the year, and the final game of O'Brien's tenure in Columbus.

Revelations about O'Brien's involvement in NCAA violations triggered the end of his standing as men's basketball coach at Ohio State.

Keels recalled how painful it was for athletic director Andy Geiger to make the change in leadership. A press conference was hastily called in June, and O'Brien was dismissed. Geiger noted how troubled and disturbed he was that "a rule was admittedly violated and that it took us five years to find out about it." The events led to a lawsuit, self-imposed sanctions, and questions about whether the program could recover.

It was hard on Andy. He was one of those athletic directors who could be very visible when things were going well. When the basketball team was in the NCAA Tournament, you would see Andy walking around during the open practices at the different tournament sites. I think he was really fond of Jim O'Brien, and when that whole thing developed and Andy had to make the change, he had asked Jim to resign, but Jim wouldn't. So they made the decision to terminate him. I know that really killed Andy. It really took a lot out of him.

The coaching search began, and many of the names that were floated as replacements for Randy Ayers seven years earlier resurfaced. One name in particular stood out above the rest. There was a groundswell for Bob Knight, who had played at Ohio State and was, at the time, coaching at Texas Tech. Knight had plenty of ties to the Big Ten, especially considering his laundry list of accomplishments as leader of the Indiana program. There were rumblings, however, that Knight would only entertain the position if he did not have to go through the interview process. It did not seem as though that would sit well with Geiger, considering the circumstances that contributed to the vacancy at Ohio State in the first place.

There was all of this buzz about Bob Knight and talk of all of these candidates. Then Thad Matta's name surfaced. I was familiar with Thad because I went to Xavier, so I had paid attention to what Xavier had done. That year, they were a controversial call away from getting to the Final Four.

Xavier reached the Elite Eight in 2004. In Matta's three years at the school, the Musketeers went 78–23 and won five NCAA Tournament games. Matta took over at Ohio State in July 2004, which made things tricky on his end with regard to recruiting and laying the foundation for his vision. In December of that year, the university announced a one-year postseason ban for O'Brien's transgressions, which Ohio State had hoped would suffice in the eyes of the NCAA. The school tacked on another year to Matta's contract, since he accepted the position despite the looming cloud hanging over the program. It also vacated its 1999 Final Four appearance.

Motivation was not always a simple task. Many of his players were holdovers from O'Brien's tenure. Matta had not recruited them. He hardly knew them. Recruits who had committed to O'Brien had to be convinced that Ohio State remained the right place for them. Matta had never seen Je'Kel Foster play, but he still wanted the junior college transfer to relocate to Columbus. Plus the Buckeyes knew that their season would end promptly at the conclusion of the Big Ten Tournament. This was not an easy assignment for a new coach.

"One of the hardest things I have ever had to do was walk in and tell guys they couldn't go to postseason play for a crime they didn't commit," Matta said, "and then motivate them on a daily basis, knowing it was going to end, and there was no chance of a reward."

Before the season began, Matta and his new staff had a tragedy to deal with that fall, as an automobile accident claimed the life of the mother of guard Brandon Fuss-Cheatham. It also left his father seriously injured. The entire team traveled by bus to western Pennsylvania to pay their respects. At the time, Ohio State's football team was playing against Michigan State in East Lansing. Before the bus crossed into Pennsylvania, they were able to find a radio affiliate that was carrying the football broadcast. Ted Ginn Jr. was having a career day for the Buckeyes, with a rushing touchdown, a receiving touchdown, and a punt return for a third score. When Ginn zigged and zagged his way through Michigan State's line of defense for the third time on the afternoon, Keels, in a bout of spontaneity, shouted out an old catchphrase from Al Bundy, the lead character from *Married…with Children*. "He went through Michigan State's defense like Mexican water through a first-time tourist!" Keels yelled.

At first, the players on the bus were not sure they had heard Keels correctly. They all looked at each other. Then, after a moment had passed, they all broke out into laughter. It provided a much-needed bit of comic relief on an emotional day.

Ohio State pieced together a 20–12 season in Matta's first year at the helm, including an 8–8 mark in Big Ten play. The most memorable moment, of course, came against Illinois in the final game of the regular season. The Fighting Illini entered that Sunday afternoon affair at the Schottenstein Center with a glistening 29–0 record. They breezed past their opponents with their sharpshooting backcourt trio of Dee Brown, Deron Williams, and Luther Head, and Roger Powell and James Augustine provided plenty of muscle in the post. The Illini would eventually proceed to the national championship game, where they lost 75–70 to North Carolina in a battle of star-studded No. 1 seeds.

The Buckeyes wanted to tarnish Illinois' regular season, though. One year earlier, Illinois had clinched the Big Ten regular season title with a 64–63 victory in Columbus in the final game before the conference tournament.

Their players and fans were filling the place, jumping up on the press table where we were broadcasting, and enjoying the moment with their many fans who had traveled to Columbus.

The Buckeyes did not forget. Fast forward to March 6, 2005, as the unranked Buckeyes battled Illinois, the top-ranked team in the nation. Daequan Cook, a potential recruit from Dayton, was in the stands as a spectator. Cook was AAU teammates and friends with Greg Oden and Mike Conley Jr., a pair of highly touted recruits. It was widely expected that the three wanted to play together in college. Cook could not have come away more impressed with what he witnessed that afternoon. He committed to Ohio State a couple of weeks later. Oden and Conley followed suit that summer.

"They took a heck of a chance on us," Matta said. "I'll be forever grateful to those kids for doing that. Without a doubt, their faith in our program and in the Ohio State University [was] instrumental."

Before the game, Keels walked into the Ohio State locker room to record a pregame interview with Matta. The two had established a great working relationship. Matta felt comfortable confiding in Keels. As Keels turned on his recording device and began his routine of asking about the upcoming game, Matta launched into an off-the-record, colorfully worded, never-to-be-aired rant that, when stripped of its locker-room vocabulary, indicated that his team—as severe an underdog as ever—would shock the world and knock off the unbeaten Fighting Illini. Both Matta and Keels were left laughing by the end of the coach's spirited tirade. Keels then restarted his recorder and taped a new answer that was more suitable for the family-friendly airwaves.

Bruce Weber's bunch really had not been tested in about a month, since an early-February win at Crisler Arena in Ann Arbor, Michigan. Their only game decided by five points or fewer was an overtime victory against Iowa in late January at Assembly Hall in Champaign. So when the Buckeyes closed to within 64–62 in the final minute and Head clanked a three-point attempt off the back of the rim, it was uncharted territory—for both teams, really. A year earlier, Matta's Xavier team ended St. Joseph's bid for an unbeaten season with a 20-point beatdown in the A-10 conference tournament semifinals.

Matta barged into Ohio State's huddle and demanded that the Buckeyes go for the win, rather than attempt to set up a high-percentage shot that could force the game to an extra period. The players were inspired and energized, but Matta had to remind them that they had yet to draw up a play. Brandon Fuss-Cheatham dribbled the ball to the center of the court, a few feet behind the arc, to set up the offense as the clock ticked under 10 seconds. Tony Stockman, the team's leading scoring guard, slipped past a double screen set by big man Terence Dials and forward Matt Sylvester. Stockman was the decoy. That left a pair of defenders glued to Dials, which allowed Sylvester to take two steps back to clear some space.

Without hesitation, Sylvester—who scored a career-high 25 points in the game—nailed a go-ahead three-pointer from in front of Ohio State's bench with five seconds remaining, and a frenzy ensued. Keels' voice shook on the radio call: "Matt Sylvester, right wing, shoots a three! Bullseye! Matt Sylvester knocks it down! The biggest shot of his life!"

We were down at the scorer's table, at floor level.
The ball was inbounded almost right in front of us.
A lot of it had to do with the charmed season that Illinois
was having. Here's a team in Ohio State that can't play in
the postseason. This is kind of their bowl game, to be able
to knock off No. 1 and an undefeated team. With everything
that had happened the previous year, with the head coach
being fired, a new coach coming in, to see it end like that,
it caught you off guard in a good way.

"It was one of those days where the rim looks as big as the ocean," Sylvester said, "and you just have that feeling that anything you throw up is going to go in. I don't know why that day was my day, but I'm glad that I was able to step up to the occasion."

Sylvester raised one index finger in the air as he sprinted down the court, Buckeyes fans jumping up and down in the stands. Powell misfired on an off-balance jumper at the buzzer, and Ohio State fans stormed the hardwood. With the postseason ban in effect, this was indeed Ohio State's Super Bowl, and the Buckeyes emerged victorious.

"We literally didn't even think we had a chance in that game," Sylvester said.

It really signaled that, maybe there's some excitement back with Ohio State basketball. That was big.

The transformation was underway.

Two years later, Matta sat at a podium the day before his Buckeyes went to war with Florida in the national championship game in Atlanta. Matta reflected on that upset victory against Illinois.

"I hope we can look back in 10 years and say that game was a pivotal step," Matta said, "a defining moment for Ohio State basketball. Without a doubt. Were we going to get those recruits anyway? Maybe. But it obviously helped us in that regard. I think it solidified Ohio State for our guys. The greatest thing that win did for us and our culture as a program, when we went into our spring skill stuff, our guys had a rejuvenated spirit about them. Our guys from that time in the spring—we had nine weeks in the quarter system, [and by] the end of June, they got so much better going into the next year that that enabled us to be picked seventh in the Big Ten, and we won the Big Ten outright. I go back to that spring and I go back to the Illinois game just for the morale boost that it gave our kids."

About a week into Matta's role as Ohio State head coach, a prominent coach at a different program told him, "You just got one of the greatest jobs in the country and nobody knows it. Take your time. It takes one recruiting class and you can build that thing."

Enter the Thad Five, the group that would push the program over the edge and complete Matta's restoration project. The influx of talent, with Oden, Conley, Cook, David Lighty, and junior college transfer

Othello Hunter, vaulted the Buckeyes into the conversation of the top teams in the country.

The day before that title bout against the Gators, five Ohio State players sat in front of microphones before a room full of reporters. Florida was aiming for its second consecutive championship, which prompted a question about the most prolific teams in college basketball history. Conley, Oden, Jamar Butler, Ivan Harris, and Ron Lewis were asked to identify the best college hoops team they could remember watching growing up.

Butler, Harris, and Lewis all selected the 1991 and '92 Duke teams that won consecutive championships. Conley chose the 1994 Arkansas team that knocked off Duke in the title game (and then finished runner-up to UCLA the following year). Oden went with the 2000 Michigan State squad, anchored by point guard Mateen Cleaves, the two-time Big Ten Player of the Year and 2000 NCAA All-Tournament selection.

Matta was later posed with the same question.

"I would probably say the 1960 Ohio State Buckeyes," he said, smiling. "No. 1, because they were wearing scarlet and gray. You look at that team, it was a young team. I'm half-joking, because I wasn't born yet, so I didn't see that team play."

He then switched his answer to the 2001 Duke team, highlighted by eventual NBA talents Shane Battier, Jay Williams, Carlos Boozer, and Mike Dunleavy Jr.

"I know they had to be a great team because they played Arizona, who they beat in the championship," Matta said. "Jason Gardner, Gilbert Arenas, Richard Jefferson, Michael Wright, Loren Woods—the bench for Arizona had four other lottery picks. That was a heck of a basketball team. The UNLV team that won it [in 1990] was awfully good as well. North Carolina [in 2005] I know was a great team because I know how good Illinois was."

With the trajectory of the program and the incoming recruiting class, Ohio State had a chance to join those heralded teams in the history books. Matta knew it, but he did not want to get ahead of himself. After all, Ohio State was just a few seasons removed from a last-place finish in the Big Ten and one season removed from a postseason tournament ban. One step at a time. The first step? Conveying to this new group that, with hard work, dedication, teamwork, and trust, the team could develop into a championship contender.

They laid the foundation in Matta's first year in Columbus, with the 20–12 season, capped by the emotional victory over previously unbeaten Illinois. The next season, a veteran Ohio State team finished first in the conference standings, with a 12–4 mark in Big Ten play. Add in five talented newcomers, and Matta had a recipe for a memorable season.

"It was a plan that was in the back of our mind," Matta said. "I really thought that we could build Ohio State. I didn't think that we could be as successful as we have been the last two years. And even winning 20 games the first year, I didn't know it could happen that fast. I give the seniors that have played for us—Ivan [Harris], Ron [Lewis], Jamar [Butler]—tremendous thanks for the trust in us. And the recruits we got, this is the vision we were selling them on: help us rebuild the Ohio State University basketball program."

Oden and Conley, teammates at Lawrence North High School in Indianapolis, were the two standouts in the recruiting class. When they committed to Ohio State, many pegged the Buckeyes as Big Ten favorites and scribbled their name beside perennial powerhouses such as Duke, North Carolina, UCLA, Kentucky, Arizona, and Kansas. Matta was quick to remind people, though, that this was not the classic case of a few freshmen joining a seasoned squad and contributing to a momentous run. This was a group of freshmen tasked with carrying the load. Butler was the only returning starter. Lewis would shift from a bench role to a starting spot. Plus, Oden missed the beginning of the season because of a broken right wrist. Since Oden would play such a profound role, Matta and his assistant coaches had to prepare for the season in two vastly different ways: one lineup and plan of attack that included the seven-footer and one that did not.

"That was kind of my big thing," Matta said. "'Do we have the ability to get to the Final Four when our center's hand won't move?'"

So, while many maintained grand expectations for the Buckeyes, Matta approached the season with much more hesitancy. He joked that every night when he drove home from a practice or a game, he would play Merle Haggard's song, "If We Make It Through December."

If we make it through December
Everything's gonna be all right, I know

The team expected Oden back by January, and knowing that they would have to endure some growing pains while assimilating so many new faces and playing styles into the system, Matta just wanted to reach the new year without any unconquerable obstacles at hand.

Well, Merle be darned, Oden returned in early December. And right away, Matta witnessed what drew him to the big fella in the first place. Oden's first collegiate game came against Valparaiso, and even Crusaders coach Homer Drew said in a pregame interview, "I think the fans are in store for something exciting today." Oden came off the bench that day for the only time in his college career. Matta first heard about Oden when the center was in middle school. He went to watch Oden and Conley play during their freshman year of high school.

"With Michael, I knew when I watched him that he would be the perfect point guard in our system," Matta said. "With Greg, as time went on watching him, you just knew that he was going to be something special with his size and his ability. When we got to Ohio State, they were obviously a huge priority. We had five scholarships to give. We didn't get the job until late. A lot of the guys were gone. That's why we were blessed to get Ron [Lewis] when we did. So we were scrambling. We actually made a risky choice in saying, 'We're going to spend a majority of our time recruiting the juniors as opposed to the seniors.' Looking back on it, I'm glad we did it."

Matta marveled at Mike Conley Sr.'s athletic ability when he was younger. He considered Conley Sr.'s dunk from the free-throw line as the greatest slam he had ever seen. Matta recalled Conley Sr. stealing the ball in the state championship game, taking off from the charity stripe and ramming it through the hoop with two hands. Matta grew up about two hours south of where Conley Sr. attended high school. Matta joked that, before he even reached high school, he declared that if Conley Sr. ever had a son, he was going to recruit him. The elder Conley starred in track and field at the University of Arkansas and later won gold and silver medals in the Olympics, as well as three Foot Locker Celebrity Slam Dunk Contests. Matta followed his career the whole way through.

When he finally watched Conley Jr. play, Matta thought, "If I can get his son and meet Mike Conley Sr., this is going to be the greatest day of my life."

In late September 2006, Matta handed each player a pamphlet. Inside the manual were guidelines for the team's academic expectations and training schedule. It also included information about the Final Four. The message was clear: if they worked their tails off, Atlanta, the site of that season's Final Four, was a possible destination. The grand stage was not out of the realm of possibility. A Big Ten championship was attainable, too. Matta hoped it would serve as motivation, though he figured the players would forget about it 10 minutes after they skimmed through it in the team meeting.

Conley recalled his first day on Ohio State's campus, when Matta was delivering his recruiting pitch. Matta showed them a video of the

Final Four and conveyed the idea that, if they committed to Ohio State, they could reach those heights.

"When he told us that, we believed it," Lewis said, "but we knew it was going to be really hard. Going through a non-conference schedule and winning, that gave us an extra boost and the extra confidence going into the Big Ten. And with everything going the right way, with Greg coming back, it just made our confidence even higher. We believed in it from the start."

The Buckeyes only suffered a couple of slip-ups during the regular season. They fell short against seventh-ranked North Carolina, 98–89, at the Dean Smith Center in the Big Ten/ACC Challenge. They were pummeled by No. 5 Florida, the reigning champion, 86–60, in Gainesville two days before Christmas. And they lost a nail biter, 72–69, in Madison against No. 3 Wisconsin in early January. Three losses—all against top 10 opponents and all away from Columbus. Otherwise, Ohio State took care of business. They unseated Wisconsin in late February after the Badgers had ascended to the top of the national polls. They had no trouble against the five other Big Ten teams that earned NCAA Tournament berths. And they conquered the Badgers a second time in the conference tournament final.

Ohio State gradually evolved into a title contender. They entered the big dance with a 30–3 record, a 17-game winning streak, and both the Big Ten regular season and tournament crowns. Matta said he had "never coached a team like this," but he liked the way his players handled having a target on their backs. It helped that they struggled in—and learned from—hostile environments in Chapel Hill, Gainesville, and Madison.

"I think you get numb to it all," Matta said.

The Buckeyes earned a top seed in the NCAA Tournament. Oden was healthy. The youngsters had handled adversity, learned from mistakes, and jelled as a unit. The path to Atlanta had come into focus. The journey that started in September was nearing its crescendo.

"I really didn't know what to expect," Matta said, when asked if he foresaw this before the season. "I thought that we could have a really good basketball team. To be sitting at 30–3 and having won 17 straight games and two of our losses are to No. 1 seeds that were ahead of us—one was without Greg Oden, the other he had been playing for three weeks, and the other was at Wisconsin—I'm pretty excited with where we are. We were a No. 2 seed last year, now a No. 1 seed this year. I think that hopefully says a lot about our program and where it's come in three years."

Ohio State breezed past No. 16 seed Central Connecticut State, the Northeast Conference tournament winner, in the opening round of the NCAA Tournament. Then came a clash with Matta's old school, Xavier, and his good friend and former assistant Sean Miller, who succeeded him as head coach of the Musketeers.

The Buckeyes trailed 59–50 with 2:54 remaining at Rupp Arena in Lexington, Kentucky. Lewis connected on a pair of free throws, Ohio State got a stop, and Butler nailed a deep three-pointer. After another defensive stop, Lewis converted a three-point play to narrow the deficit to one with a minute and a half to play. After a couple of Xavier free throws, Oden split a pair of his own.

While Oden was sidelined with a broken wrist early in the year, he taught himself to shoot free throws left-handed. When the team wrapped up the Big Ten regular season title, it had nearly a week off until its next game. During that time, Oden practiced shooting free throws in his normal fashion. For a guy who averaged nearly 16 points, 10 rebounds, and more than three blocks per game, the most impressive thing Oden accomplished, in Matta's mind, was shooting free throws with his off-hand as a means of staying productive during his absence.

"I think the other thing," Matta said, "would be along the lines of sitting out for seven straight months and being thrust into the pressure situation that he was thrust into and everybody expecting him to be 100 percent from the day he got back and how he handled that and how he continued to work. He rode the peaks and the valleys and just was extremely diligent. Every day after practice, he would spend about 40 minutes working with [assistant coach Alan Major] and just developing his game. You think of the frustration—we've laughed about this—when he came back, he was rebounding with one hand. He was catching with one hand. He couldn't use his right hand and people at times would criticize him, and we were laughing as a staff, saying, 'They have no idea what he can't do.' We didn't want to tell anybody, because we didn't want to exploit that weakness for Greg. Now his hand is much more mobile, and I think those have probably been the most amazing things."

The Buckeyes failed to score while down by two, and Xavier's Justin Cage stepped up to the line. A pair of free throws would all but seal Ohio State's fate. Cage made the first. The second free throw spun around the rim and landed in Harris' hands. The Buckeyes hurried down the floor. Conley handed off the basketball to Lewis in the middle of the *K* in the massive, blue UK logo at midcourt. Lewis took one dribble, squared up, and fired. He drained the three-pointer with two seconds remaining to knot the score at 62–62. Xavier's Drew Lavender missed a desperation heave from three-quarters court, and the teams headed to overtime. Ohio State marched to a 78–71 win in the extra frame and advanced to the Sweet 16.

Lewis had his shining moment. He had more than enough validation for his decision to transfer to Ohio State, but this was the perfect cherry on top—you know, other than a national championship. Matta never scouted Lewis when he attended high school in Columbus or when he started his college career at Bowling Green.

"A couple of coaches lost their jobs over that," Matta said, laughing. "Honestly, I am embarrassed to say we didn't know who he was. He played on such a great high school team. But in watching him develop, I think that you've got a very passionate kid who wants to be a great player.

He wasn't a great shooter when he came to Ohio State. He could drive the ball and get fouled. But I think he's really added a lot to his game and his assist-to-turnover ratio has gotten a lot better."

Matta cited Foster, a starter on the 2005–06 team, as having a profound influence on both Lewis and Butler. Foster mentored his younger teammates, even when Lewis was redshirting. In practice, Foster helped to get the most effort out of Lewis and Butler.

The decision to transfer to Ohio State was simple for Lewis.

"I knew he had been winning since he became a coach," Lewis said. "And I also knew that he played the style of basketball that I would like to play. So those two go hand in hand with each other. I made my decision off of that."

The decision was pretty easy for Ohio State, too.

"He didn't have to sell very hard," Matta said, "because we didn't have very many players. We needed to fill scholarships. We were like, 'If he can walk and chew gum, we'll take him.' Obviously, when the fax comes through and Ron Lewis is transferring, we were like, 'Oh, who is this kid? He plays at Bowling Green.' I think we had some tape. We talked to his high school coaches, talked to some guys who were in his league, and sat down and talked with Ron. As I always do, I want to know what's important to the young man, what he's looking for, and make sure it's a fit. There was no question that it was a great fit for us and for him coming back home. It obviously worked out well.

"From the day Ron came to Ohio State, he's had an incredible work ethic. The reason he came to Ohio State is he wanted to compete at this level. To see this happen for him, I couldn't be more excited. Ron really came to grips with a phrase we have: 'The more you give, the more will come back to you.' To watch his play elevate, I'm not surprised. I'm happy that it has. Obviously, he's made some big shots for us. He's done it really throughout his career for us. Him being a senior on this team, leading these guys, I couldn't be happier with the job he's done."

Lewis' shot propelled the Buckeyes to the Sweet 16 for the first time since that magical 1999 run. A reporter asked Matta what was going through his head when the ball dropped through the net. Matta responded that he was concerned with how much time was remaining on the clock. The answer, of course, was two seconds, and anyone who blinked likely missed the fact that the game was headed for an extra period.

The reporter followed up by saying, "You have to be kidding me," amazed at the fact that Matta did not take any time to celebrate or wipe the sweat from his forehead. Matta had his reasons, though. He flashed back to the 2000 NCAA Tournament, when he was an assistant coach for No. 12 seeded Butler to a one-point lead against No. 5 seed Florida in the closing seconds of overtime in a first-round matchup in Winston-Salem, North Carolina. The Gators corralled a missed Butler free throw, and Mike Miller drove to the basket and tossed up a wild shot as he stumbled to the floor. The ball bounced in at the buzzer and before Miller could get up, his teammates piled on top of him. Florida ended up reaching the championship game, in which it ran out of steam against Michigan State. Matta said he thinks about that game every day, including the fact that Lavall Jordan, an 81 percent free-throw shooter, missed a pair of freebies in crunch time. Head coach Barry Collier turned to Matta and asked if they should call a timeout. Matta rejected the idea, saying there was no need to ice their own shooter. It didn't matter. (Butler, by the way, ended up meeting No. 1 Florida in the Sweet 16 of the 2007 NCAA Tournament. The Gators won by eight.)

"I've often told people that that probably propelled my head coaching career," Matta said, "because they kept showing that shot over and over, and Collier went to Nebraska because Florida did so well. I was standing there as the next Butler head coach."

The Buckeyes moved on to San Antonio for a date with Tennessee at the Alamodome. Matta had never been to San Antonio, so the night before the game, he awarded his team an hour and a half—okay, technically, it was an hour and 23 minutes, since, as the coach explained, he granted them permission to leave their team dinner at 8:37 PM and they had a mandatory film session at 10:00 PM—to explore the city. Matta moseyed down the boardwalk on the banks of the San Antonio River. Some players visited the Alamo and took pictures.

This was a dangerous Volunteers squad that ranked ninth in the nation in points per game. Juniors Chris Lofton and JaJuan Smith combined to average 36 points per contest. And Smith buried an uncontested three-pointer four seconds into the game. It was time for the Buckeyes to buckle up. This was going to be a fast-paced affair with plenty of outside shots. In fact, about two minutes after Smith's opening bucket, Harris, Lofton, Lewis, and Smith—in that order—all nailed shots from beyond the arc in a span of 43 seconds. A 20–6 Tennessee run, with most of it coming after Oden picked up his second foul, spurred Bruce Pearl's team to a healthy lead. Lighty converted a three-point play in the final second to slice the halftime deficit to 49–32.

At the first official TV timeout, when Tennessee had already drained four three-pointers, Matta reminded his team that the Volunteers came out firing in similar fashion in their previous game against Virginia. Tennessee eventually cooled down and hung on to win by three. With about five minutes remaining in the first half, after Tennessee had mounted a 17-point advantage on Ohio State, a few players said to Matta, "I thought you said they were going to cool down."

"I had the thought in my mind at one point during the first half," Matta said, "if they play like this, they're going to win it all. The foul trouble, we were disheveled. We never got into a rhythm or flow. And quite honestly, they punched us so hard, we were at the nine count. David's play at the end of the half was a little bit of a momentum boost for us. It cut it to 17. Boy, we were really jacked up going into that halftime."

Matta told his players in the locker room that they needed to toughen up and fight back, that they needed to play with more aggression, that they did not put forth the proper effort in the first stanza. He didn't like his team's body language, saying they "went in wounded." He talked about the plan to chip away at Tennessee's lead, to rise to the occasion defensively and focus on getting easy baskets on offense. Conley noted that guys' heads were down at halftime, that they sorely needed to rally together.

"If you fall apart," Conley said, "there's going to be no good from that."

"We saw their body language coming out for the second half and we knew we had to attack," Lewis said. "Our main focus was to get to the basket, get free throws so we could stop the clock and knock down shots. Their body language was like they already had the game won. We just had to come out with aggressiveness like they did in the first half."

Ohio State opened the second half with a 12–2 run, and all seemed right again. The Buckeyes finally took their first lead of the game with about eight-and-a-half minutes remaining. Conley split a pair of free throws to hand Ohio State an 85–84 edge with six seconds left. Tennessee's Ramar Smith gathered the second attempt after it bounced off the back of the rim. Smith drove the length of the floor and offered up a last-second shot, but Oden swatted it away to the baseline. The Buckeyes could breathe again. Years later, when Oden returned to Ohio State to complete his degree, he said he just *had* to make that defensive play because he "just wasn't ready for the season to stop."

"I think if you look up in the dictionary 'living dangerously,' my picture would be plastered right next to it," Matta said. "I think it's funny, in this tournament, the two most important words are *survive* and *advance*. And we've been very, very fortunate the last couple games to do those two things. I'm proud of our guys—half pissed off at them for how we started. But we came back in the second half and were able to make the plays down the stretch to win the basketball game and advance."

Oden was limited to 18 minutes of action because of foul trouble, after he had fouled out of the Xavier game the previous weekend. Matta said Oden was "a little bit down" after that. Against Tennessee, he was called for three personals in the first half and picked up his fourth with about 11 minutes remaining in the game. But he was able to stay on the court to deliver the most important defensive contribution of the evening.

While the officials have a very tough job and can be easy targets at times, it was very telling that after the Ohio State–Tennessee game, none of the three officials who worked it were around for the regional finals. In fact, three men who were not in San Antonio for either semifinal game were brought in for the Ohio State–Memphis matchup.

Oden arrived in Columbus with plenty of fanfare as a five-star recruit carrying the expectation that he would stay in school for only one year before bolting for the NBA as a top draft pick. He certainly made his presence felt when the spotlight was brightest.

"Everybody forgets," Matta said, "they think the notoriety and publicity started when he got to Ohio State. It's been following him for three years. He's such a great kid. He doesn't like it, he doesn't want it. And I think his teammates picked up on that and appreciate the fact that he is who he is. And I think that's made things better. One of the biggest things that we've tried to change in our time at Ohio State is the culture and environment of our program. We preach family. We preach togetherness. And I think all the guys have done a great job at that."

Oden kept a level head. He obliged with his media duties, even though he knew there would be a constant barrage of NBA questions that he preferred not to answer. There was one instance in which he sat in one of the coaches' offices and said, "Please don't make me go back down there and do more [interviews]." Other than that, Oden handled the attention with class. Matta recalled how, after Ohio State knocked out Wisconsin to win the Big Ten Tournament title, he tried to gather his players to talk to them, but he could not find Oden. The big man was still on the court, signing autographs for about 50 little kids.

"He wasn't going to leave until they all got his autograph," Matta said. "That's who he is. He knows what comes with it, and I think he handles it tremendously well."

The NCAA Tournament does not allow for much time for reflection or recovery. Two days after the frantic finish against Tennessee, Ohio State had to battle 33–3 Memphis. Matta entered his hotel room at one point for about 10 minutes, and his wife asked him if he wanted to take a stroll along the Riverwalk.

"I guess my look answered the question for me," Matta said, "because she then apologized for asking the question. I'm so in love with this team, and I want them to be successful, and I feel like we have to put all of our efforts into getting them as prepared as we can physically and mentally. I hope at some point later than sooner, I will be able to sit down and really enjoy it, because it has been an incredible run. At some point, I hope that I can sit down and really go through it, as I do in the off-season, sit down and watch all the game tapes again. I think I'll see some things that will really make me smile."

Ohio State did not need any last-minute heroics to fend off Memphis in the regional final matchup. The Buckeyes sank 35 of 41 free-throw attempts to march past the Tigers 92–76 and secure a spot in the Final Four. As the team cut down the nets after the game, fans at the Alamodome chanted, "One more year! One more year!" They knew Oden and Conley were likely headed to the NBA whenever this special run reached its conclusion. So they later switched their tune to, "Two more games! Two more games!" A couple of victories would notch the program its first national title since 1960.

That's a big deal, even at a place like Ohio State, where football reigns supreme each year and basketball often takes a back seat, no matter the degree of success it achieves. Even as the Buckeyes navigated their way through the NCAA Tournament in 2007, they did so while losing a bit of attention to spring football. That never bothered Matta during his tenure in Columbus. He appreciated the resources the athletic department could provide and the enthusiasm the fan base showered upon the teams from the stands.

"Football has been one of our greatest tools," he said. "The one thing that it taught me as I attended my first football game here was the passion that our fans have for the Buckeyes. Coach Tressel has gone above and beyond the duty of helping us along the way. He's been a sounding board for me. He's pointed me in the right direction on numerous occasions. I believe that we can have both here. You point to a Florida, you point to a Texas—that ultimately was what I was striving to do. I think the big thing for me is I don't wake up every day and say, 'My goal is to make this a basketball school.' I don't want to do that. I just want to put the best product on the floor. Knowing that our guys this year made it to the [Final Four], the [football team] won the national championship in 2002, I think, quite honestly, we can have both. Also, I think that speaks volumes of what the Ohio State athletic program is all about."

Ohio State would meet Georgetown in the national semifinal matchup. The winner would play the winner of UCLA/Florida. The Hoyas had ended the Buckeyes' season the previous year, as No. 7 seed Georgetown upset No. 2 seed Ohio State in the second round of the tournament in Minneapolis. As Matta met with the media the day before the game in 2007, he noted how the last time he was sitting behind a microphone at the Georgia Dome, his 2004 Xavier team had lost a closely contested game to No. 1 Duke with a Final Four berth on the line.

The first stages of the tournament were a whirlwind for the Buckeyes, with late comeback victories against Xavier and Tennessee, and a quick turnaround before a hard-fought win against a physical Memphis team. Matta was exhausted by the time the Buckeyes arrived in Atlanta, and while he was thrilled with his group's exploits to that point, he wanted to make sure they did not settle.

"I take great pride in the kids and the work ethic they put in," he said, "but we don't want to be a team that checks off who made the Final Four and get our rear ends kicked. We have to keep getting better."

Matta recalled watching Final Fours with his dad when he was a kid. Father and son would sit on the couch and watch the Monday night title game every year. Matta was eight when Bob Knight's Indiana team cruised to the national championship with a 32–0 record. Scott Eells, a freshman forward on that team, hailed from Matta's hometown of Hoopeston, Illinois. Now the Buckeyes were one of the teams the entire country was tuning in to watch.

"I'm just living a dream," Lewis said. "It's a loss for words. I never thought I'd be in this position. With hard work and a great team behind you, you can do anything. When I first went to Bowling Green, I never had any option of transferring at all. But I was unhappy. I tried to make my move somewhere where I could be happy. And coming on with Coach Matta was a great thing, because he's been winning for so long. I made my move, and great things are happening."

The meeting with Georgetown was billed as a battle between big men, with the 7' Oden opposing the 7'2" Roy Hibbert. Which team could most consistently feed its center? Which big man could demonstrate more might in the paint? Which seven-footer could turn away any naïve ball handler who considered it wise to drive to the basket? Well, there was not enough conclusive evidence to answer any of those inquiries. Oden picked up two fouls in the first three minutes of the game and spent the rest of the first half on the bench in spectator mode. Hibbert was assessed his fourth foul with the score tied with 8:49 remaining. From that point, Ohio State went on a 7–0 run. The Hoyas never climbed closer than four points after that.

The Buckeyes had Conley to thank. The point guard submitted one of his most effective showings of the season, with 15 points (on 7-of-12 shooting), six assists, and five rebounds. He stayed on the floor for all but one minute of the game.

"He's one of those guys, a classic example," Matta said. "As a coach, you want him to do really, really well because he is, every day, the last one to leave the practice floor. He has his routine before practice. He has his routine after practice, where he's going to get his shots up. He's going to do his ball handling. He's going to do all of those things. And I think that that is gratifying to me, to see a kid working as hard as he does, to progress as well as he has."

Matta hugged each of his players after the win, which sealed the Buckeyes' spot in the national title game. As he embraced his freshmen—who by that point had played and experienced enough to shed the traditional first-year-player label—he thanked them for "believing in us, and believing in the vision that we had." Butler noted how, when the group of freshmen arrived on campus, they were hungry to learn and to pick the brains of the veterans on the roster. Keels made his way to the locker room after the game to record a brief interview with Matta. The coach revealed that, in the midst of the postgame hoopla, Oden had asked if Kyle Madsen, a backup center who was sitting out the season after transferring from Vanderbilt, could join the locker room celebration with the rest of the team. Oden was appreciative of the work Madsen had done in battling Oden in practice all season.

"To have those guys," Matta said, "I feel blessed. What they have meant for our program, the winning mindset that they have brought with three [high school] state championships, all the AAU championships that they have won—I've said this: you spend time with those guys, they make you better people. Obviously, they make me a better coach."

So the Buckeyes, a team loaded with talent, but short on experience, an ongoing work in progress because of youth and injuries, had peaked at the proper time. And now a rematch against Florida awaited. Ohio State was a much different team when the Gators humbled them by 26 points in Gainesville in December. A lot changed in that time. Oden's wrist fully healed and he worked his way back into playing shape. He, Conley, Cook, and Lighty all gained invaluable experience in big games, in tooth-and-nail conference games, by winning the Big Ten Tournament and by squeaking past a few tough opponents in the big dance. And a team with plenty of new faces and new playing styles learned how to most effectively mesh on the court.

In that December 23 meeting, the teams were tied 40–40, with 17 minutes remaining. Florida then went on a 31–7 run over the next 10 minutes. "They blitzed us," Matta said. "They were making shots. They were getting stops. They really took the game to another level. We weren't mentally ready to get in the fight with them. I think that it was one of those games. I think every team has one. Florida beat us. I mean, they beat us good down there. The thing that we've hopefully learned from it is—and you see every game in the NCAA Tournament is a game of runs—you have to be able to withstand that mentally and physically and keep your composure and keep the fight to execute the game plan. We just weren't able to do that down there."

Why did Ohio State agree to that game in the first place? What good could it have served to face the defending champions in their venue two days before Christmas? The Buckeyes knew that they would be aligned with North Carolina in the Big Ten/ACC Challenge. They figured that, by adding one other daunting road game to the schedule, they would be equipped to handle the rigors of the Big Ten conference schedule. The Buckeyes came up short in both contests, but Matta contended that it helped the team build some character and gave the players some difficult experiences to draw from, which could pay dividends down the road.

Of course, Ohio State would have preferred to play a different opponent in the national title game. They did lose to Florida by 26 points, after all. And while there was a sense of revenge on the mind of Ohio State's players, they knew this was going to be a tall order. Florida was aiming to become the first repeat champion since Duke turned the trick 15 years earlier. They returned the exact same starting lineup from their previous championship season, as players bypassed a chance at the NBA for the opportunity to repeat as college kings.

"I don't want to say that, you know, I circled Florida and said, 'I want to play Florida again,'" Matta said. "You get beat by 26 points, you really don't want to see that team for a while. But I do think that I wanted to be in this position and I was a realist and that there was probably a really, really good chance that Florida was going to be the team that was going to be on the opposite side, and so be it. If we were playing UCLA or anybody else that was coming out of that region, it was going to be a great opponent. But I never have said to myself, 'Boy, I want another crack at Florida.'"

I remember that day, thinking, "Ohio State is playing in the national championship game...in basketball." For the first time since '62. In what was Thad's third year. It had you thinking that some more good things were coming for them.

To the team, it was a chance at history, and it just so happened to be against a familiar group of opponents clad in blue and orange. To Buckeye Nation, though, it represented much more. The Gators had dashed Ohio State's championship dreams on the gridiron three months earlier. This was a shot at redemption, an opportunity to foil what seemed like a storybook script, just like how Florida buried the Buckeyes' bid for an unbeaten season with a 41–14 beatdown in Glendale, Arizona.

Tressel and Matta spoke after Ohio State knocked out Georgetown. The two communicated often. At that point, Florida had yet to emerge victorious against UCLA, so there was no dialogue about the Buckeyes-Gators cross-sport rivalry. Tressel expressed his pride for the basketball team's run to the title game. Matta often leaned on Tressel for advice, for guidance in how to lead a program at such a distinguished university with such a passionate fan base.

Tressel, though, would occasionally send his responses to Matta in the middle of the night. After he received a text from Tressel at 3:00 AM, Matta wondered if the football coach ever slept. Without warning, Tressel visited with the team and gave a speech during the NCAA Tournament when Ohio State was playing its early-round games in Lexington.

"He's always offering up words of encouragement," Matta said. "It says a lot about him. It's all focused on team and playing hard and trying to finish a mission, and it's always good to get those [texts] and read and ponder them and take it and let the guys know what he said."

The second go-around against the Gators went a bit better, but Ohio State still came up on the losing end. The Buckeyes shaved Florida's 14-point advantage to six with five minutes remaining, but they never inched closer than that. Entering the game, there was a widespread opinion that the Gators were the better team, with more veteran players, a deeper lineup, and more size down low. When Ohio State players were asked about that consensus the day before the game, they all offered a similar answer.

Butler: "They're a great basketball team."

Harris: "They're an excellent team."

Well, except for Lewis.

Ohio State center Greg Oden slam-dunks in the national title game versus the Florida Gators on April 2, 2007, at the Georgia Dome in Atlanta.

"They're a good team," he said. "You know, people pick them to win the game. People thought we were going to lose [to Georgetown], but we came out on top. It's nothing new to us."

A few minutes later, Lewis was asked to expound on his choice of words when describing Florida.

"They're a good team to me," he said, with a smile. "That's all I can say about it."

After another few minutes of questions directed toward Matta and his players, another reporter asked Lewis why he considered the Gators to be "good" instead of "great."

"They're a good team," Lewis repeated, again with a smile. "I go, bad team, middle team, and then a good team. That's the top. So, if you want a great team, you look at the [Chicago] Bulls."

Matta was not afraid to use the word "great," and he resorted to some damage control to make sure Lewis' words did not provide Florida with any bulletin board material.

"Ron's definition, I think he clarified, 'good' is 'great' to him," Matta said. "I think we're playing a great basketball team. I understand why people would give us no shot in this game on paper. I think that they are excellent."

They certainly proved it. They notched an 84–75 victory, even though Oden avoided foul trouble enough to log 38 minutes. In that time, he totaled 25 points, 12 rebounds, and four blocks against Florida's army of big men in Al Horford, Joakim Noah, Chris Richard, and Marreese Speights.

"I would put them in a category of probably one of the best teams to win," Matta said. "You're going to see those guys playing a lot of basketball for many years ahead."

All four post players proceeded to the NBA following their stints at Florida. Oden, of course, became the No. 1 overall draft selection by the Portland Trail Blazers. Conley, who had pledged to return for his sophomore season, ended up leaving for the NBA as well. His stock had soared during the NCAA Tournament, and the Memphis Grizzlies nabbed him with the fourth overall pick. That placed the finishing touches on an illustrious chapter of Ohio State men's basketball. It all began with Cook sitting in the stands, watching Sylvester bury a three-pointer to dash Illinois' dreams of a perfect season. An unparalleled recruiting class followed and paved the way for an unforgettable run to the national title game.

CHAPTER 5
A TIME FOR TRANSITION

With Ohio State readying for its first dance with the College Football Playoff, Urban Meyer thought about a few of the veteran players on his roster. He thought about tight end Jeff Heuerman and linebacker Curtis Grant. Their journeys in Columbus began in 2011, during a tumultuous time of transition, one that made the team's march to the 2014 national championship seem like a far-fetched fantasy.

"The question was never about the quality of player at Ohio State," Meyer said. "It was never the quality of coach at Ohio State. It was chemistry within the team and, obviously, distractions. And I can see an incredible sense of pride on those guys, because we talk about legacy and I talk about it all the time: there's a common thread, probably at every university, where—you see the 1968 Ohio State Buckeyes come back because they won a title. And you see the Big Ten champions come back. The bad teams, you don't ever see them come back. You don't see the former players. When you devote four years of your life and your body to a university, you want to be able to bring your son or daughter back some day and say, 'This is where your dad played.' So I feel an incredible amount of pride, not so much because I wasn't there, our staff wasn't there, but for the players that were part of the transition period—there's an incredible amount of pride."

Ohio State's football program was not accustomed to struggling or to being mired in mediocrity. The Buckeyes' 6–7 showing in 2011 marked the team's first losing season since 1988, when John Cooper oversaw a 4–6–1 finish in his first year at the helm.

Consider Jim Tressel's annual record as head coach in Columbus:

2001   7–5
2002   14–0
2003   11–2
2004   8–4
2005   10–2

2006 12–1
2007 11–2
2008 10–3
2009 11–2
2010 12–1

During that time, the Buckeyes appeared in three national championship games, three Fiesta Bowls (including the 2002 championship game), the Rose Bowl, and the Sugar Bowl. They were ranked first or second in the nation at some point in six of the 10 seasons, and they finished seven of the 10 seasons ranked in the top five.

In 15 seasons as the head honcho at Youngstown State, Tressel amassed a glowing record of 135–57–2, with four Division I-AA national championships to his credit. At Ohio State, he compiled a mark of 106–22, with seven Big Ten titles, and—of utmost importance to those who reside in the Buckeye State—a 9–1 mark against rival Michigan.

Tressel's original plans centered on coaching in the high school ranks. He later aimed to follow in the footsteps of his father, Lee, who coached for 23 years at Division III Baldwin-Wallace College in Berea, Ohio. Jim Tressel, though, never left the college level after he graduated from Baldwin-Wallace in 1975. He coached at Akron, Miami (Ohio), Syracuse, and Ohio State before he assumed the position of head coach at Youngstown State in 1986.

Following his tenure with the prolific Penguins, he edged out Glen Mason for the head coaching vacancy in Columbus and immediately endeared himself to the Ohio State fan base. "He set up Michigan as a top priority," said Ohio State football historian Jack Park, "and he followed through with that."

Tressel intended on his first year serving as a transition from one regime to the next. Ohio State went 7–5, including an Outback Bowl loss to South Carolina for the second consecutive season. "The thing I wanted to do was create a plan and then develop relationships," Tressel said. "And then, of course, you wanted to win some games along the way. But I wanted to create a plan for a culture and a set of expectations and get to know the kids and have them get to know me and make sure they knew how much I cared about them on and off the field."

That season, Tressel established the foundation for the championship campaign that followed in 2002. After lackluster seasons of 6–6, 8–4, and 7–5, the Buckeyes notched the first 14–0 season in Division I college football history.

"These kids were so hungry," Tressel said, "because they had been here, many of them three, four, five years and really hadn't had an Ohio State–type season. There was a group of…seniors who were not going to leave here without having an Ohio State season. And then the ball bounced right a couple times, and our guys kept fighting and it ended up being a good deal. When you end a year like we did in '02, with that group that had transitioned together and had grown to love one another and compete like crazy, it was a little bit melancholy after the game, the fact that we were never going to be together in that fashion."

Said Park, "I don't think the most avid, unrealistic Ohio State fan that thinks, 'We're never, ever going to lose again,' in their wildest dreams would have thought that they would go 14–0 in their second year under Tressel."

Ohio State would not repeat that sort of magical season under Tressel, but the program reached heights not seen since Woody Hayes roamed the sideline in Columbus. Another year, another BCS bowl game. Another year, another win over Michigan. Another year, another conference title.

And then, it all fell apart.

About two weeks before the 2011 Sugar Bowl, reports surfaced that a handful of Ohio State players had exchanged autographs, memorabilia, and gear for tattoos, all of which qualified as an NCAA violation.

The players were permitted to participate in the Sugar Bowl—a 31–26 Buckeyes victory which was later vacated—but they were suspended for the first five games of the 2011 season.

Now, the NCAA can vacate all the games that it wants. Those games still happened. No matter how much time Ohio State fans spent drinking hurricanes and hand grenades on Bourbon Street in the days leading up to the Sugar Bowl, they at least remember being there, even if the memory is a little hazy. And their ticket stubs can prove it. The game happened. Ohio State won. There is a box score and everything. Those to-be-suspended players all contributed. Quarterback Terrelle Pryor was named the game's MVP, with 221 yards through the air and another 115 on the ground. Dan "Boom" Herron rushed for 87 yards and a touchdown. Receiver DeVier Posey hauled in a touchdown. Even defensive end Solomon Thomas sealed the win with a last-minute interception of Razorbacks gunslinger Ryan Mallett.

So every Ohio State fan who made the trip left with some memory of a thrilling victory…or of something else. Keels knew of a couple of female Ohio State fans who engaged in some verbal jabbing with Arkansas fans at a bar on Bourbon Street. The Big Ten–SEC war had waged on all week in New Orleans, and it may have reached a crescendo with this one instance. One of the women said to a male Arkansas fan, "You know the difference between women from Ohio and women from Arkansas? Your girlfriend is a Snickers bar away from 300 pounds." The bar owner ultimately asked the two women to leave the bar for spewing their insults. The culprit told her parents that they would be proud of her for getting thrown out of a bar on Bourbon Street for taunting the opposing fan base.

The Sugar Bowl indeed happened. There are, uh, memories to prove it.

Of course, a harsh reality would quickly set in for the Ohio State football program after the bowl victory. Little did anyone know in early

January 2011 that the program would receive a facelift just a couple of months later.

As Tressel reflected on his 10 years as Ohio State's head coach, he stressed the relationships he had constructed with players and how those stood out above the win totals and bowl game trips. "I've got a whole box sitting right across from me on the counter of about 15 rings," he said. "But you know what? Those things, the dust is on them. They are just memories. But the progress a person makes, even if they stumble and fall individually and as a group, what's important is at the end of the day, they are ready to go out in this competitive world and see if they can battle their way through this tough, tough world."

How fitting.

When Tressel took to the podium the day before the Sugar Bowl, he recounted the first BCS bowl game from his tenure at Ohio State. He had arrived at the first press conference before the 2003 Fiesta Bowl in his track suit. Miami head coach Larry Coker was wearing a coat and tie. Tressel joked that he hoped the photographers would not use the "nine million pictures they took." That Sugar Bowl would end up being his final game at the helm at Ohio State.

"I think adversity, whether it's for a football team or for an individual or for those who aren't football players, is always the greatest teacher," Tressel said that day at the podium. "Not always the most fun. But always the greatest teacher. I think it does give you an opportunity to be inwardly reflective and all of those things. And I think I've been around bowl situations where sometimes I was worried that everything seems like it's too good, and all of a sudden you might get shocked at the adversity you face on the field. We've been a part of moments where we've had to handle some adversity. But, nevertheless, as we move closer to game time, [it's about] our ability to handle adversity and play together and stay together.

"You'd like to think that you can gain from those adverse situations. Not that you want them to occur in hopes that you can learn from them—but you would hope that will be the case maybe in this game—but more importantly, down the road for individuals and teams in the future."

Tressel joined the list of the suspended in March, when he received a two-game ban and a $250,000 fine for failing to notify the university of the players' transgressions. He had been made aware of the players' dealings via email but never passed the word along to anyone in the athletic department or at the university. Tressel apologized to Thad Matta for overshadowing the basketball team's accomplishment of being named the No. 1 overall seed in the NCAA Tournament. Tressel later enhanced his own suspension to five games to match the punishment his players received.

Tressel's statement read as follows:

> I request of the university that my actions now include five games so that the players and I can handle this adversity together. I spoke with [Gene] Smith and our student-athletes involved and told them that my mistakes need to share the same game sanctions.

At the Sugar Bowl, Tressel had this exchange with a reporter:

Reporter: How confident are you that the suspended players will keep their word to you and return for next season? And has anything happened to maybe make you believe any differently?

Tressel: I'm totally confident. Totally.

It all unraveled fairly quickly. Ohio State planned to retain Tressel until the backing for such a measure deteriorated and external pressure grew. Smith, the athletic director, voiced his support for Tressel for the few months the coach was under siege.

"Our intent was to retain him as our head coach," Smith said. "When you look at his body of work and what he accomplished, you look at this one action and try to take that in total perspective. I felt that it was the best thing for the kids who he had recruited to his program and who were here."

But on Memorial Day 2011, it all came tumbling down. The university "sought and accepted" Tressel's resignation. "The brand of the institution was now at stake in a greater form," Smith said. "We were constantly under attack, and so when I sat down with him that Sunday night and had that conversation, there was no hesitation on his part when I asked him for his resignation.

"I kind of understood it for a while as I first looked at it. I said, 'Okay, I see that.' But obviously, the infractions are sitting right in front of you, so I couldn't get by that. You have a responsibility as an NCAA member to ensure compliance. To make that decision on your own without at least bringing it to me or university general counsel, I have a hard time with it. I was totally shocked and surprised and really disappointed when I first heard of his decision and saw the emails. Every single level of emotion went through me. I was dumbfounded as to why he would make a decision on his own and not share that information and ask for help."

Typically on such a holiday, the local radio station outsources its local programming to whatever is being broadcast on the national airwaves. On this day, Keels had to drive to the station and cohost five hours of Tressel-related programming, taking calls from furious, shocked, and disappointed Ohio State fans, and trying to wrap his head around the disheartening end of the coach's decade in Columbus.

Luke Fickell, who was to coach the team during Tressel's suspension, was elevated to the role of head coach for the season. Instead of serving his five-game ban, Pryor bolted for the NFL Supplemental Draft, leaving backup Joe Bauserman and true freshman Braxton Miller to anchor the most important position on the field. Ohio State hosted

Miami (Ohio) in its season opener at the Horseshoe, and ESPN broadcast the game, with Dave Pasch and Urban Meyer on the call. Keels checked in at the media gate at the same time as those two. He had known Pasch for years, but had never spoken to Meyer. Of course, he had no idea that Meyer would wind up taking over in Columbus a few months later.

It was a messy season, one that ended with a Gator Bowl loss to Florida and a losing record overall. This was not foreign to Keels, who called plenty of win-starved University of Cincinnati seasons. He can recall the Bearcats' 81–0 drubbing at the hands of Penn State in State College, Pennsylvania, in 1991.

You're still getting a chance to do something that you enjoy. It still means something to listeners. What you think about in those situations is there are still people listening. There are still guys out there playing. There is still the possibility that you could see an incredible play, that you could see a player do something that sparks the start of an outstanding collegiate career. Like the Braxton Miller touchdown pass to Devin Smith against Wisconsin—you don't see those kinds of plays that terribly often.

The majority of people listening are Ohio State fans, but there are probably casual fans listening. You still have to do right by them in describing what's going on with the game. It's still Ohio State football, and it still means a lot to people, even when they aren't being as successful as most people want. We're still trying to do all of those serviceable items. But you do notice the difference. You feel the difference in the attitude of people, the atmosphere.

It really hit home for Keels when he arrived at Ohio Stadium on November 19, 2011, for a matchup between the Buckeyes and Nittany Lions. Instead of Jim Tressel vs. Joe Paterno, the old, classic battle, it was

Luke Fickell vs. Tom Bradley. That will forever stand as an easy-to-stump piece of trivia. Paterno had been ousted at Penn State 10 days earlier.

Ohio State fell short against Michigan the next week, 40–34, its first loss against its nemesis since 2003. There had been rumblings that the university would target Meyer, an Ohio native, as its next head coach. The school announced the hiring on the Monday after the Michigan game. Meyer was supposed to be part of ESPN's telecast of the game, but he requested off so as not to stir the pot even more.

University president E. Gordon Gee had formed a search committee that included Smith; Ohio State vice president and general counsel Chris Culley; executive vice president for advancement and special assistant to the president Jeff Kaplan; and two trustees—Alex Shumate and Robert Schottenstein. Smith presented the group with a list of candidates to discuss, and they ultimately whittled it down to Meyer. They valued his integrity and his leadership skills. They lauded his results at Bowling Green, Utah, and Florida. They marveled at his recruiting performance and his potential to capitalize on Ohio's rich football soil. They appreciated his Ohio roots, having been born and raised in Ashtabula, and having worked under Earle Bruce in Columbus and at Colorado State. They also were encouraged by the fact that, when Meyer stepped down at Florida after the 2010 season, he was able to take a deep breath and "reflect back on the experiences that he has had to allow him to form the leadership skills that he has."

"We're the total sum of experiences in life," Smith said at Meyer's introductory press conference. "He is, without a shadow of a doubt, one of the premier leaders in football. It's represented in his record. But more importantly, it's represented in him, the man."

Meyer was not introduced at an Ohio State–Michigan basketball game. He did not offer any promises that evolved into guarantees of an Ann Arbor destruction. He was straightforward with his mission statement, though.

"Our objective is simple," Meyer said. "It's to make the state of Ohio proud, [and to] recruit student-athletes who will win in the classroom and win on the field. I'm going to go about and try to assemble the best coaching staff in college football. Our goal is to compete and win Big Ten championships."

Meyer's father, Bud, passed away about two weeks before Meyer was introduced as Ohio State's head coach on that late-November day in 2011. Meyer identified his father and Bruce as the two most influential figures in his life. In fact, Bruce spoke at Bud's funeral.

"Every step of my career, every part of my family life, Coach Bruce has always been there," Meyer said.

Meyer described the two men as having similar personalities: no-nonsense, hard-working, family-oriented.

When Meyer made the decision to step away from coaching, he placed a new emphasis on family, which had taken a backseat during his later years in Gainesville, when his perfectionism and inability to pump the brakes spiraled out of control. He believed that he had coached the final game of his career when he left behind the Gators program. He quickly realized he missed the profession, even as his scheduled filled up with analyst work at ESPN, appointments at his kids' sporting events, and family dinners. But he pondered ways he could return to college coaching without putting a strain on his health and his relationship with his wife and children. He realized that he did not want to be the sort of coach who slept in his office overnight and missed out on his son's baseball games and his daughters' volleyball matches. The balance between work and life had completely tipped in the wrong direction. He obsessed over the former and ran out of time for the latter. So he ultimately decided that the Ohio State gig would be the only opportunity he would entertain, and he would strike a healthier balance if he landed the job.

"At Florida, I went through stages," Meyer said. "I will be the same guy [from] the beginning of the tenure. And that was a guy that did have balance, a guy that took care of himself, a guy that did not try to get involved and change everything. I think as it rolled on, we were dealing with magical things there. I call it the pursuit of perfection. I think, at the end of the day, we all know there's no such thing. I fell victim to that. I've been to a place [and] I'm not going to go back. I'm sure there are a lot of people in this room who have been places they don't want to go. And I was there. I'm not going back."

Before he could put pen to paper on his new pact with the university, Meyer's kids forced him to sign a contract that mandated he enact strategies to maintain more balance in his life. He said it was "tougher than any other contract I've signed in my life."

"This is an age-old problem," Meyer said, "about the executive or the doctor or the lawyer or the teacher, the professor, the policeman that just gets so enamored or so consumed by their profession that they forget really what the purpose of our whole deal is, and that's to raise a wonderful family. That's part of the issue we deal with today, is when you see people too consumed with their profession, and they let things go at home and then that costs them down the road."

Fickell coached Ohio State in the Gator Bowl and joined Meyer's staff as a co–defensive coordinator. It was a bit of a process, though. Meyer expressed how he wanted to hire the best position coaches the country had to offer. Meyer thought highly of Fickell from their first meeting in the spring of 2006. He watched closely as Fickell was tasked with guiding the Buckeyes through the awkward, distraction-filled aftermath of the tattoo scandal and Tressel dismissal. Meyer called some of Fickell's past colleagues for a scouting report. He watched film of Fickell's defenses at Ohio State. And the night before Meyer was introduced as the Buckeyes' head man, Meyer and his wife, Shelley, dined with Fickell and his wife, Amy, for more than three hours. The Meyers discussed the decision later that night and when Meyer rose the next morning, he looked to his wife for assistance with the final answer.

"She's a better judge of talent than I am," he said, "and there's no doubt I wanted him to be part of this team."

Meyer and Fickell met for coffee that morning at 7:00. Meyer offered him the job. Fickell accepted it, smiled, shook his new cohort's hand, and called Amy.

"It was a very good moment for Ohio State," Meyer said.

As Meyer started to assemble his staff, some of the members of the previous regime started to wonder where they stood. Some accepted jobs at other schools. Some latched on with Meyer's crew. The coaches who were not going to be retained were required to leave behind their key cards when the team traveled to Jacksonville for the bowl game. They were to coach the game, but could not enter the football facility upon their return to Columbus.

More than anything, you felt for the people involved. There was some obvious tension among some of the coaches who were being kept and who weren't being kept. There are coaches and their families and you feel for them and some of the players, not knowing what their situations are going to be.

Meyer cherished his two seasons on Bruce's staff at Ohio State in the mid-'80s. He can recall how Bruce would lose his mind and slam his hat to the ground when he thought that Bo Schembechler was receiving preferential treatment from the referees. When he spent the 2011 season in the broadcast booth for ESPN, Meyer returned to Ohio Stadium with Pasch and Chris Spielman—who played linebacker for the Buckeyes when Meyer was on staff—to call a game, his first trip to the Horseshoe in more than two decades. He reminisced about how, when he was a graduate assistant, he would sneak out of the old locker room when there were 16 minutes remaining before kickoff to watch the marching band filter onto the field. Bruce would be making his final preparations and Meyer would sprint down the stairs and marvel at the band as it paraded onto the grass.

As he sat in the broadcast booth, high above Ohio Stadium, and the band stormed out of the tunnel and onto the field, Meyer wiped tears from his eyes.

"All the memories came back," he said.

Meyer was raised on Ohio State football when he grew up in Ashtabula, on the eastern side of the state. He wore No. 45 on his jersey as a kid in honor of Archie Griffin, the great two-time Heisman Trophy–winning tailback at Ohio State. He can recall shopping with his mom around Thanksgiving when he was little and hearing loud speakers blaring throughout the town, airing the broadcast of the Ohio State–Michigan game. It was Woody Hayes vs. Bo Schembechler, an installment of the renowned Ten-Year War. Meyer was hooked. His entire town shut down. Friends and relatives gathered together to watch the rivalry game each year. No one milled around town on that Saturday afternoon in November.

"That's the game of games," Meyer said. "That's the game that I grew up watching."

His first involvement in the game came in 1986, when Michigan quarterback—and now head coach—Jim Harbaugh guaranteed a victory over Ohio State and a trip to Pasadena for the Rose Bowl. Harbaugh proved clairvoyant, as Michigan ruined Ohio State's sunny Saturday afternoon with a 26–24 triumph. In Meyer's second year on staff at Ohio State in 1987, the Buckeyes returned the favor and beat the Wolverines in Bruce's final game as Buckeyes head coach.

Bruce had been fired by university president Edward H. Jennings earlier in the week, which triggered protests from the fan base and displeasure from the players. Kicker Matt Frantz sealed the victory with a fourth-quarter field goal. Prior to kickoff, Jennings told Frantz to suggest to the defense to think of his face if that would light a fire under the team and potentially contribute to a win. It apparently did just that. The Buckeyes wore headbands as a show of support for their coach. The players carried

Bruce, clad in a suit and tie and black fedora, off the field. Bruce repeatedly pumped his fist as fans filtered out onto the field to celebrate.

"That was satisfaction, seeing how happy he was," Spielman said. "We can all look in the mirror and walk out of here proud. For a man to go through what he went through this week, to hold his composure is the sign of a true man, a true Buckeye. He may not have all the charisma. He may not have all the personality. But there is no better football coach in America."

That coach has served as a mentor to Meyer for decades. And Bruce, of course, had Woody as his mentor. Meyer met Woody once at the ROTC building on campus, where Woody had his office. Meyer and his wife, Shelley, were attending a recruiting dinner at the Scarlet and Gray golf course at Ohio State when he was a graduate assistant under Bruce. Woody was in a wheelchair, and there were about 30 people lined up to greet him. Shelley asked if they could join. Meyer replied that he would bring her over to his office sometime. He never got the chance. Woody passed away on March 12, 1987, at the age of 74.

"I still regret that to this day," Meyer said. "So does she, that she never had a chance to meet Coach Hayes. A 'fan' is not a strong enough word. To think I admired him, yes—there has always been a portrait in my house of Coach Hayes. It goes back real thick, real strong, the admiration I have for Coach Hayes and Coach Bruce."

Meyer raved about his time in Florida, where he directed the Gators to a pair of national championships and played a role in transforming the SEC into a perennial powerhouse. He referred to the six years he spent in Gainesville as a "dream job." But he knew there was a special connection to where he spent his youth, where he studied under Bruce, and where he ended up after taking a year off to regain some perspective.

"This is my home state," Meyer said at his introductory press conference, which came two days after his hometown shut down for yet another Ohio State–Michigan battle. "And it's great to be back home."

The 2012 season should have been another year of transition. It should have been Meyer getting to know his team and his players grasping what he expected of them. It should have been a new coaching staff growing together, learning what worked and what did not work. It should not have been a season that ended with a zero in the loss column, even with a bit of a soft schedule. It was not always pretty. Ohio State squeaked by Michigan State in East Lansing, 17–16. It snuck past unranked Indiana in Bloomington, 52–49. The Buckeyes needed a last-gasp score to force

Ohio State quarterback Braxton Miller breaks free for a big gain in the Buckeyes' 26–21 victory over Michigan in 2012, completing their perfect 12–0 season.

overtime in a 29–22 win against unranked Purdue in Columbus. They also required an extra period to knock off Wisconsin in Madison, 21–14. But they kept winning.

It was the intensity of Urban and his coaches that they passed down to those players. It started with Urban. They wanted to make winning that division championship a big deal. It was the only thing they could win, but it was a way to try to really reward those players who bought into what it was that they were doing, and it planted the seeds for the start of his tenure there. It was amazing.

The Buckeyes had a postseason ban, so the Michigan game would serve as the final piece to the undefeated puzzle. They were ineligible for the conference title game and were forced to watch bowl season in their sweat pants and from the couch, with a bag of potato chips in hand. Ohio State will always circle Michigan week in black Sharpie and then highlight each day of that week with the brightest, blinding shade of yellow that Office Max has to offer. But an 11–0 team hosting Michigan and not having any bowl-game hierarchy to worry about, meaning only the Wolverines stood in the way of an unbeaten season in Columbus? Yeah, that should be enough motivation for the Buckeyes.

That game is a season unto itself. In a year like that, that had to be good ammunition for those coaches. This definitely was going to be the last game of the year. You could really make what has been a strange season end on a really good note. And every year, no matter what their records are or anything, it's just big because it's Ohio State and Michigan. There is always a lot of sizzle to that week, just because of the rivalry.

The Buckeyes hung on for a 26–21 victory to complete the imperfectly perfect season and put the rest of the country on notice. Meyer did not come to Columbus to mess around. He wasted no time in restoring confidence in the program. No transition year necessary.

That made it far from surprising, then, that Meyer and Ohio State captured a national championship just two years later, despite the hurdles the team had to clear to attain it. There was no gradual build to Meyer's reign at Ohio State: the Buckeyes went 73–8 in his first six years at the helm. They carried an unblemished record into the Big Ten title game in Indianapolis in 2013, when Michigan State spoiled their season. Indianapolis was merely supposed to be the layover on Ohio State's trek to Pasadena for the national championship game and a date with heavyweight Florida State. Meyer spent much of his postgame media session with his head down, his team's program-record 24-game winning streak over.

"It's going to haunt all of us, I imagine, for a little while," Meyer said.

Ohio State converted only once on 10 third-down opportunities. They went 0-for-2 on fourth-down tries; the first failure, in which the Buckeyes opted to try a Miller rush instead of a handoff to workhorse back Carlos Hyde, all but secured the victory for the Spartans. Miller completed only eight of his 21 pass attempts. That does not create a recipe for success, and Michigan State—which scored the game's first 17 points—completed the 34–24 upset.

That was a head-scratcher. It had a lot of people thinking. They had trouble throwing the ball. The Michigan State secondary was called the no-fly zone. At the end of the game and for a while afterward, you just wondered, would things have been different had they given the ball to Hyde rather than run Braxton Miller?

"It sucks," said Corey Linsley, a senior center on that team. "It's a reality check. We hyped them up a little too much. They're obviously a good team, but it was like we were playing the Bears or something. We were looking for everything and then we settled down and realized we had to do what we had been doing all year."

The toughest part for Meyer was that, this time, Ohio State actually had postseason permission. There were no bowl game restrictions. A trip to the national title game legitimately hung in the balance, a tantalizing reward for a team that ran the table the previous year but had no such end-of-season incentive.

"I really wanted these guys to experience something special," Meyer said.

They would the following season. The 2011 season was painful, but only like a bruise, not a broken bone. The program healed quickly. Meyer won two national titles at Florida. It only took him three seasons—and who knows how the Buckeyes might have fared had they been eligible for postseason play in 2012—to capture his first Crystal Football in Columbus.

"In 2006, that's still probably the most special [one] because that was the first one," Meyer said. "That was a group of kids—the Brandon Silers of the world, the Dallas Bakers of the world—we're forever attached. The second one was a great team, a team that was the best team in America pretty much start to finish after [a loss to Ole Miss]. This was a team that kind of came out of nowhere. To start comparing this one versus that one, that will never happen. Is there a little zest to it [since] I grew up in the great state of Ohio?"

Meyer reflected on how guys from his high school showed up in Dallas the night before the championship game against Oregon. They reminisced about their days in grade school, when they rooted for Ohio State. Meyer noted how meaningful it was to coach the team that his own high school coaches and childhood friends and siblings had cheered for for decades. He continued. "It's very, very special."

And the program that sunk to a rare low in 2011 had returned to the great heights it had grown accustomed to over the previous decade.

The scandal and Tressel's missteps had retreated deep into the recesses of everyone's minds. Ohio State was on top again, and the future looked mighty bright. Recruiting, the lifeblood of any strong college football program, has always been Meyer's bread and butter. And now he had it served to him on a silver platter.

"The door's open," Meyer said. "You move to the front of the line."

Meyer was sitting with assistant coach Kerry Coombs after the Buckeyes won the 2014 championship and told him, "Man, I can't wait to go out recruiting. If you can't recruit to this now, you're officially a bad recruiter. And not just because of the championship. There's just so much going on in our program right now on the positive side. It's not theory. It's testimony."

Meyer's Ever-Growing Coaching Tree

Earle Bruce planted the seeds for Urban Meyer's coaching career. Little did Bruce know what sort of majestic coaching tree would bloom. Meyer cites Bruce as the greatest on-field influence in his life. It certainly was not Meyer's playing career that paved the way for him to become one of the most decorated coaches in college football.

"Playing experience? I was a professional baseball player, which doesn't really help much in this arena," Meyer said. "And I went and played college football and had a very mediocre-to-below career."

The Atlanta Braves selected Meyer, an infielder, in the 13th round of Major League Baseball's 1982 amateur draft out of St. John's High School in Ashtabula, Ohio. Meyer spent two seasons at the organization's rookie league affiliates, one-and-a-half in Bradenton, Florida, and half a season in Pulaski, Virginia. All together, Meyer batted .182 with one home run in 44 games as a minor leaguer. He did draw 22 walks, which boosted his on-base percentage to a respectable .321. His .264 slugging percentage was not major league material. He also committed 10 errors.

Meyer attended the University of Cincinnati, where he played cornerback and earned his degree in psychology. He shifted to Ohio State for his master's degree in sports administration. There, he served as a graduate assistant on Bruce's staff for two years.

"It started when I became a graduate assistant at Ohio State, worked for Earle Bruce, and got a taste for major college football," Meyer said. "And the biggest thing [is] that I have had the experience that not many coaches have. I have worked for incredible mentors. I have worked for Earle Bruce and Sonny Lubick and Lou Holtz and Bob Davie, and they are all tremendous friends. But there are bits and pieces of our program [at Ohio State] that I have taken from those great leaders. And that has been more important for my career...who I have been able to work with and for."

After his stint on Bruce's staff in Columbus, Meyer spent two seasons as an assistant coach at Illinois State. From there, he reunited with Bruce at Colorado State, following Bruce's controversial dismissal from Ohio State. Meyer lasted six seasons as the wide receivers coach at Colorado State before he relocated to South Bend, Indiana, to assume the same role at Notre Dame under Holtz and then Davie.

In 2001 Meyer earned his first head coaching job at Bowling Green. In two seasons at the Mid-American Conference school, he racked up a 17–6 record. The year before he took over, the Falcons had amassed a 2–9 mark. After his two seasons with Bowling Green, he took the head coaching job at Utah. His two seasons with the Utes went even better. In 2003 Utah went 10–2, with a 17–0 win in the Liberty Bowl against Southern Miss in Memphis. The next year, Utah went undefeated, with a sparkling 12–0 record, capped by a 35–7 drubbing of Pitt in the Fiesta Bowl. Utah became the first team from a non-BCS conference to reach a BCS bowl game. Meyer and Kyle Whittingham acted as co–head coaches for the bowl game, since Meyer was bound for Gainesville to fill Florida's head coaching void.

Meyer amassed a 65–15 record in six years with the Gators, highlighted by a pair of national championships. His Florida teams won five of their six bowl games. In his first six years at Ohio State, Meyer posted a 73–8 record, including a 47–3 mark in Big Ten play. The Buckeyes claimed the national title in the inaugural College Football Playoff in January 2015.

Along the way, Meyer has developed his own coaching tree. Assistants do not tend to last long when serving on his staff. They often get better jobs, and sometimes, head coaching jobs, elsewhere. Meyer listed a handful of former assistants who blossomed under his watch:

- Dan Mullen, a graduate assistant at Notre Dame when Meyer coached there, a quarterbacks coach under Meyer at both Bowling Green and Utah, and an offensive coordinator and quarterbacks coach at Florida, served as the head coach at Mississippi

State for nine years before moving on to the head coaching job at Florida at the end of the 2017 season.

- Charlie Strong, the defensive line coach at Notre Dame when Meyer was there and the defensive coach on Meyer's staff at Florida, has since been the head coach at Louisville, Texas, and South Florida.
- Kyle Whittingham has directed Utah's football program ever since Meyer bid farewell to the school at the end of the 2004 season.
- Gary Andersen coached the defensive line at Utah in 2004 and later served as the head coach at Utah State, Wisconsin, and Oregon State before returning to Utah in January 2018 as an associate head coach and defensive assistant.
- Tim Beckman was an associate head coach and defensive coordinator at Bowling Green during Meyer's tenure there and later became the head coach at Toledo and then Illinois.
- Dan McCarney spent three years as an associate head coach and defensive line coach on Meyer's staff at Florida before he became the head coach at North Texas.
- Doc Holliday served as an associate head coach, safeties coach, and recruiting coordinator at Florida and, since 2010, has been the head coach at Marshall.
- Tom Herman was Ohio State's offensive coordinator for Meyer's first three seasons in Columbus before he advanced to the head coaching position at Houston and then Texas.
- Steve Addazio graduated from an offensive assistant at Florida to the head coach at Temple and, since 2013, Boston College.
- Chris Ash, Meyer's co–defensive coordinator for two seasons at Ohio State, has captained the Rutgers football program since December 2015.
- Gregg Brandon oversaw the offense at Bowling Green before he succeeded Meyer as head coach of the Falcons.

- D.J. Durkin was Meyer's defensive coordinator at Florida (and a graduate assistant on his Bowling Green staff) and, since December 2015, has served as the head coach at Maryland.
- Luke Fickell, a longtime Ohio State assistant, took over as head coach of Cincinnati in December 2016.
- Mike Vrabel, a defensive assistant on Meyer's staff in Columbus, became the Tennessee Titans' head coach in January 2018.
- Everett Withers, an associate head coach and co–defensive coordinator for Meyer's first two seasons at Ohio State, moved on to the head coaching role at James Madison and later at Texas State.

"So very proud of them," Meyer said. "We stay in contact, and I just think it's great that I have never had an offensive coordinator stay more than two or three years."

CHAPTER 6

WOODY, BO, AND THAT TEAM UP NORTH

Paul Keels attended Archbishop Moeller High School in Cincinnati, a football factory that produced plenty of future Buckeyes, including Rob Murphy and Sam Hubbard (not to mention a couple of prominent Reds players in Hall of Famers Ken Griffey Jr. and Barry Larkin). Keels once walked out of school and headed toward his 1966 Mercury Comet Caliente in the parking lot, and there he was, walking alongside football coach Gerry Faust (who later coached at Notre Dame and at Akron), headed toward the practice field:

Woody Hayes.

It was almost like everybody stopped. There was like a holy figure who had come to our high school.

Keels never officially met Woody, who was there with his recruiting hat atop his head.

Just standing there, seeing him. I never met him, but I obviously was very aware of him and having known people who played for him, it was a unique experience that day in high school, just seeing him in our parking lot of our practice field.

Woody was a master at recruiting. Just ask former quarterback Bill Long.

"He's the best recruiter," Long said, "maybe in the history of sports. He got so personal, with not only the athletes, but the families."

He typically got what he wanted. Woody joined Long and his parents at a high school basketball game during the coach's courting of the quarterback. Long did not want to commit to Ohio State that night. He had never traveled on an airplane. He dreamed about playing the field, about jetting across the country to schmooze with other suitors who wanted him under center. He hoped to fly to Wisconsin and to

Colorado. He planned to visit Northwestern. He really wanted to milk the process, so he would have to stave off Woody's bid to secure his commitment that night.

At halftime of the basketball game, Woody welcomed Long into his office. The two sat down at the coach's desk and Woody pulled out a vocabulary book.

"Okay, Bill," he said. "I'm going to go over some words with you right now."

Long was a bit puzzled. Was this an English quiz or a meeting with a college football coaching legend?

"Adjacent," Woody said. "Spell *adjacent.*"

Long offered up the *a* and the *d* before he tripped up. Woody interrupted to correct him.

"No, Goddamnit," Woody said. "That's not right. It's *a-d-j.* You should know by now, Bill. Now, give me the definition of *adjacent.*"

Long, still confused by the point of the exercise, submitted a response.

"Now, use it in a sentence," Woody demanded.

This back and forth persisted for the entire second half of the basketball game. Finally, the coach closed the book and shot straight.

"Okay, let's get down to business," Woody said. "I know you want to come to Ohio State. Let's get this over with and commit tonight."

Long hesitated. He told Woody that he was "95 percent sure" he wanted to attend Ohio State, but he said he was not quite ready to make the arrangement official. Woody seemed to accept that answer. The two rejoined Long's parents in the gymnasium.

"I felt like I beat him," Long said. "I was walking on air."

This was far from Woody's first recruiting rodeo, of course. He had his recruit precisely where he wanted him. The four went out for dinner at a restaurant down the street. Woody spotted Ritter Collett, a writer and editor for the Dayton *Journal-Herald.*

"Ritter, you know Bob Long and his wife, Shorty," Woody said. "We're recruiting their son, Bill Long. Ritter, Bill has something to tell you."

Long's eyes opened wide. His jaw might as well have been resting on the floor.

Woody did it. That sly, shrewd, calculated coach. A recruiting mastermind. How did he pull it off?

Long had no choice but to supply the statement Woody wanted.

"Yeah," Long said. "I've decided to come to Ohio State."

Long did not come to regret that decision. He appreciated Woody's involvement in the process.

"At all of the other schools, assistants did everything," Long said. "You only saw the head coach right before you went home. They were just above it. But not Woody."

Woody continued to exert effort in the process, even after he heard the sweet sentence of commitment. Long had planned to major in art at Ohio State. Before Long officially enrolled, Woody summoned the high school senior to his office. He asked Long to lug some of his artwork with him. When Long arrived, Woody picked up the phone on his desk and dialed Ohio State's fine arts department.

"I want a meeting with one of your people over there," Woody said. "I have a recruit who is interested in art, and I want you to take a look at his work."

Long was blown away by how invested Woody was with his prospective players. That sort of care endeared him to his players and to those who knew him best, despite his reputation as the surly emperor of Ohio State football.

A voyage to Caldwell, Ohio—about two hours east of Columbus— reveals even more about the root of Woody's personality. No one in the tucked-away town had seen or spoken with Woody since he landed a punch on Clemson's Charlie Bauman in December 1978, resulting in his dismissal from the university and the end of his coaching career.

When word spread that Woody was coming to visit, everyone quickly got on the same page: no one was to bring up the incident. After all, who knows how Woody would react? He was not one to sugarcoat his thoughts, and Caldwell was the place where he escaped Ohio State, escaped football, escaped his reputation. In Caldwell, he read books in solitude in his private cabin in the woods or read books to the children in the small town.

Woody always stopped by the Saling residence on his visits to Caldwell. He admired Gennie Saling's work ethic. She plucked worms off the tobacco on her family's farm and tossed the burrowing bodies into a can. She milked cows, tended to horses, completed housework for her neighbors, served at each of the three bars in town, and worked at a steel plant, where she knew how to operate every machine in the building. When Woody was away, Gennie mowed the lawn surrounding his cabin. He would call her to say he was coming to town and would stop by the Saling household to exchange his dirty clothes for clean garb.

Gennie knew that her husband, Ed, the man who had built Woody's cabin, lacked a filter between his brain and mouth. So she warned Ed, "Don't you say anything to him about that."

Naturally, upon Woody's arrival, Ed approached the coach and, without a second thought, inquired, "What the hell can make a man do that?"

Oh, Ed.

When Woody died in March 1987, Gennie still had some of his clothes hanging upstairs in her house. Her grandson has one of Woody's patented button-up, short-sleeve shirts framed in glass and hanging on a wall in his house.

Caldwell is home to several branches of the Hayes family tree. And even to those in the area who are not related by blood, Woody was like family.

"He never forgot to come back," said Mabel Schott, Woody's second cousin.

A twisting road, 10 miles long, winds through the small town, with no stoplight in place to halt anyone's progress on the way to Woody's cabin. The sights along the way are antiquated—you feel as though you are traversing a trail straight out of a 1950s film—with rusty, downtrodden cars sitting among dauntingly tall weeds and untamed grass. There's a ceramics shop, a bar, and an inn that each sit atop dirt lots. Cows and horses roam about massive pastures that occupy the vast real estate between homes.

A hidden pathway peeks out just before a sharp left turn on the main road. A rusty gate hangs ajar at the beginning of a leaf-covered trail that leads up a hill to Woody's old hangout. Layers of white- and brown-stained wood compose the framework. Two wooden benches—one of them with a busted limb—nearly span the width of the porch. Woody often settled onto one of the seats and wrote. He authored a book about football, which Melinda Antill, one of eight Saling children, had in her home. The stone chimney appears to be begrudgingly separating from the foundation of the cabin, as the old mortar in between hangs on for dear life. A cluster of barren wasp nests dangle from the track that lines the front door.

Woody installed a red sink and a gray bathtub to treat the place to some Ohio State decor. He placed an Ohio State rug beside the front door. The lodge includes a fireplace, a living room, a kitchen, a bathroom, and a bedroom loft. Melinda was fond of the Easter lilies that bloomed each spring all throughout the woods that encompassed the yard.

On Saturday afternoons during the summer, Woody would walk up the street to the bar owned by his cousin. He would buy drinks for everyone in the building. He was familiar with every patron at the three bars in town, and, of course, everyone knew Woody. An Ohio State adornment hangs from Mabel's white front door.

Here was this imposing figure who represented one of college football's premier programs, a seemingly callous coach who was dismissed for striking an opposing player during a bowl game. Yet in Caldwell, where he spent his childhood summers on his grandparents' farm and his off-season weekends in his private log cabin, Woody conformed to a simple, innocent manner of life.

"I liked to talk to him," Mabel said. "He was really understanding. He liked everybody."

In Columbus, Woody played the role of daunting dictator.

"He was always in control," said former Ohio State coach Earle Bruce, who replaced Woody at the helm upon his firing.

Bruce recalled how Woody would often drive alone, but on the rare occasion in which he served as a passenger in someone else's vehicle, Woody would control the radio, the position of the windows, and the heat and air conditioning.

Really, though, Woody was a bit of a recluse. Bruce said his old friend would go mountain hiking by himself fairly often.

"He was always kind of a loner in that respect," Bruce said.

In Caldwell, Woody was a hallowed figure, revered for his five national championships and his sustained success, but just as respected and beloved for his generosity. "Nobody was intimidated by Woody Hayes around here," said Melinda, who passed away in December 2017 at the age of 62.

The fact that he tended to steer conversations away from his own legacy played a part in that. "Never once did that man ever talk football," said Gennie, who spent all 92 years of her life in the area before she passed away in July 2017. "All he ever talked about was learning and working."

When Woody swung by the Saling residence on Sundays, he would present the adults with a case of beer and the children with a watermelon. He would sit in a chair in the living room and preach the importance of education to the children, grandchildren, and the rest of the kids in the neighborhood. Woody told them to focus on their schoolwork and on the significance of learning and that, without an education, football was meaningless. They had all heard the tales about Woody making his players stay at his house under his watchful eye until they improved their grades.

"I was told that if they weren't making their grades, you did not want a teacher giving him a phone call," Melinda said. "If he got a phone call, you were dead meat."

Once a year, Woody sent tickets to the residents of Caldwell. They filled a car or two to make the 105-mile trek west to Columbus and sat in the front row to watch their hero captain the perennial championship contender. "My kids, they used to go to school and tell people they met Woody Hayes," Gennie said. "Kids didn't want to believe them."

The first time Woody brought his wife to Caldwell, Gennie was nervous. She pictured Woody's wife as some model of elegance and grandeur, a high-class, hoity-toity snob of sorts. She feared she would not be able to relate.

And then, Anne stepped out of the car.

"Here she comes," Gennie recalled, "this little, old, heavyset lady who had her hair back in a bunch like a farm lady. She was just like a farm lady, too. She was the nicest person that you could meet." They hit it off. And once Woody died, Anne would mail Gennie $100 each Christmas.

"He was a very good-hearted person," Melinda said. "It was amazing how good he could be to people. If anyone needed something, he would definitely help you." That is what made is so difficult for Ed to fathom what Woody did during the waning moments of the 1978 Gator Bowl against Clemson. Besides, he and Woody never shied away from speaking their minds to each other.

So Ed asked, "What the hell can make a man do that?"

And Woody replied, "They ticked me off!"

That was the extent of the conversation.

"You'd just have to know Woody," Melinda said. "He had a temper. There's no doubt about that."

They knew Woody better than most. They certainly knew him better than Keels, who was more familiar with the other coach involved in the vaunted Ten-Year War.

Keels can remember people flying planes with banners that read, "Fire Woody." That, of course, was prior to 1968, when Woody's Ohio State team ran the table, with an unblemished 10–0 record and a championship-crowning victory against No. 2 USC in the Rose Bowl. Keels compared the longtime Buckeyes coach to Oklahoma's Bud Wilkinson, who directed the Sooners from 1947 to 1963, and Texas' Darrell Royal, who led the Longhorns from 1957 to 1976.

He certainly was a legendary figure.

Keels worked in Detroit for seven years, first calling Pistons games for WJR. He switched stations and, for the next six years, served as a play-by-play announcer for University of Michigan football and basketball games. There were five stations that carried Michigan's games at that time, from Detroit to Ann Arbor to Flint. Don Canham, Michigan's athletic director, permitted anyone to broadcast the games so long as they paid the rights fees. During that time in the 1980s, there were five groups that were paying the rights fees.

Keels first called Michigan games in 1981, but because of the abundance of broadcasting teams, he was not able to develop the same sort of relationship with the head coach that he could once he relocated to Columbus. Still, Keels was always in attendance at Bo Schembechler's weekly Monday press conference during the season. He would hear Bo tell old tales about Woody and about Ohio State, about the rivalry between the two Big Ten adversaries. Bo would sit with the writers and radio and TV personalities while they chowed down on lunch. Once they

Woody Hayes (right) and Bo Schembechler shake hands on the field.

finished their food, they would stick their cameras and microphones in Bo's face to record their video and audio.

Keels was not on a first-name basis with Bo, but the coach would recognize him when the two crossed paths, especially at Michigan basketball games. That is where Keels secured the most face time with Bo, who would walk past Keels' seat to get to his own.

Keels can recall that he was at a shootaround session for Ohio State basketball at the Schottenstein Center when he first heard that Bo, a former Ohio State assistant coach, had passed away on November 17, 2006, the day before the No. 1 Buckeyes hosted the No. 2 Wolverines in a matchup between 11–0 juggernauts that was hailed as the Game of the Century.

The game featured a 3:30 kickoff, a rare deviation from the normal noon start time for the meeting between the rivals. As a result, it was dark by halftime. Heading into the contest, there was plenty of debate about the game's stakes. The winner would certainly punch its ticket to the national championship game, but might the loser deserve a bid as well? Should there be an unprecedented rematch, or would that tarnish the meaning behind the mid-November affair? What if there had been a conference championship game in place on the schedule at the time? How would that have impacted everything?

In my lifetime, I remember in the early '70s, there was a Thanksgiving Day game between Nebraska and Oklahoma that they called "The Game of the Century" for a long time. I don't know that there has been another one like that. The 2006 game really did stand alone in a lot of ways, and the fact it was such a good game helped the image of the whole rivalry.

The Buckeyes held on for a 42–39 victory to pave their path to Glendale, Arizona, for the BCS title game. The teams traded jabs, with big play after big play, but Michigan could not mount the necessary fourth-quarter comeback. Troy Smith amassed 316 yards through the air, with four touchdown passes, which helped to overshadow Michigan running back Michael Hart's 142 yards on the ground and three scores.

A couple of other Ohio State–Michigan games stand out to Keels.

The 2002 game. It kind of cleared the decks for Ohio State. Michigan probably played better than everybody thought they would in that game, and it went down to the final play.

The other one that stands out to me was in 2005 in Ann Arbor, when Ohio State came from behind and Antonio Pittman scored the game-winner on the last drive. Troy Smith threw the ball to everybody. He converted a big running play and a pass to Anthony Gonzalez. That win was big, because it really got them rolling. It took them into that Fiesta Bowl with Notre Dame that they won. It got them rolling into 2006, to where they ended up being that team that went to the national championship game.

Urban Meyer tends to wax poetic about the Ohio State–Michigan rivalry, in which he has played a leading role in recent years. Before he commenced his official coaching career, Meyer worked as a graduate assistant under Bruce at Ohio State. The Buckeyes were playing in Ann Arbor in 1987 and Meyer had one important task on his plate.

Both teams come out of the locker room through the same tunnel to get to the field at the Big House. Meyer was assigned to stand in the way to keep the Ohio State players from filtering out onto the field before the Michigan team. So there stood Meyer, a 23-year-old graduate assistant tasked with holding back a sea of revved-up meatheads when he peered across the hall at the Michigan locker room and saw Bo with a collection of the biggest guys he had ever seen. Bo just glared back, leaving Meyer to think, "What am I doing here in this situation?"

As Urban likes to say, "Who are you to be here?"

When Meyer told the story, he revisited his first real in-person exposure to Bo and recalled how Bruce would go crazy about how he believed Bo got a lot of leeway from the officials to rant and rave on the sideline. When Meyer became the head coach at Bowling Green, Bo reached out to him. Bo knew he had been a graduate assistant for Bruce and he appreciated that. The kind gesture meant a lot to Meyer, who does not open up too often, but does have an affinity for well-respected coaches.

When presented with the notion that he might share some traits with Woody, a sly grin sweeps across Meyer's face. He plays it off as though he has never considered the comparison, but that cannot possibly be the truth. Meyer coached under Bruce, who coached under Woody. Bruce sees some resemblance between his predecessor and his prodigy. To those familiar with both men, some of the similarities in style, demeanor, and authority are striking. Jim Otis, who played fullback under Woody from 1967 to 1969, even texted Meyer and told him as much after Ohio State beat California in September 2013.

"He does have a little bit of Woody in him," Otis said. "He coached with Earle, and Earle is a disciple of Woody's, so you're going to get a lot of Woody. There's a big difference between Earle and Woody, but Urban has that."

No one wanted to tweak or disturb Woody. He hired Rudy Hubbard to coach the team's running backs, but Woody actually presided over the position group. When Hubbard asked to design plays for the backs, Woody shot back, "Well, what do you think I'm going to do?"

"These guys were afraid to pick out a movie the night before a game," Long said, "because Woody might not like the movie."

As Hubbard put it, "[Woody] could have you scared to death and at the same time make you love him for the fact that he cared about you. I just saw that as Woody being Woody."

Meyer might not appear as hardened or unreasonable or as difficult to approach, but he still demands respect in a similar fashion. The two coaches also share a commitment to their craft that borders on obsession. Meyer stepped down at Florida to escape the mounting stress that took a toll on his health and family. After a year away from the field, he relocated to Columbus, but only after he signed the famous pink contract devised by his daughters that mandated he balance his time and energy more effectively.

Woody endured similar coaching rigors, which explains why he occasionally fled to his cozy cabin in Caldwell. Long said Woody "sacrificed family and everything for his job."

"He had a single-minded approach to everything, and that was football," said Larry Catuzzi, who coached under Woody from 1965 to 1967. "His life, other than his military career, was football. And he devoted all of his time, at some expense to his family, I thought, to football."

Meyer did list three of Woody's values that he, too, treasures: love and care for the players, demands of the players, and placing a premium on academics.

"He's pretty tough," Otis said, "but he's fair and he's good to the kids. He will fight for them all the way, and that's how Woody was. When it comes down to nut-cracking time, they're going to fight for him. He's got some of that in him and he should."

Hubbard, a tailback at Ohio State from 1965 to 1967, hosted a poker game in his dorm room one night. A few teammates and a couple of non-players gathered together and dealt cards and smoked cigarettes. The sound of a few knocks at the door struck fear into Hubbard. He could sense that the Czar of Columbus, known to periodically check in on his players to make sure they were studying, was standing (and probably fuming) on the other side of the door.

Woody ejected everyone from the room but Rudy. He heaved an ashtray at the wall, sat Rudy down, and warned him that if any other authority caught him pulling this sort of stunt, he would have been dismissed from the football team. Hubbard was terrified, but also a bit proud that Woody cared. The two had almost nothing in common when it came to fashion, politics, or personality, but they grew close over the years.

"When I think back about it," Hubbard said, "I think there was something about me that he liked all along. I just never knew what it was."

Hubbard landed in Columbus in 1964 with dreams of following in Jim Brown's shifty footsteps, with a prolific NFL career and all of the glory that came with it. However, at Ohio State, Hubbard spent most of his time blocking for Jim Otis, Paul Hudson, or Bo Rein. In his final game in 1967, Hubbard rushed for 103 yards and two touchdowns in a victory against Michigan in Ann Arbor. At last, he performed how he knew he always could had he just been handed an opportunity—and handed the football. Catuzzi, sensing Hubbard's frustration, asked him after the game, "You're glad to be leaving here, right?"

Hubbard thought his bond with the Buckeyes football program had come to an end. His playing career was over and it was time to advance to the next stage in life. When his high school held a banquet that winter to recognize his college feats, Hubbard unveiled his animosity toward the program before friends, family, and former classmates in the audience. He was disenchanted. He thought he would have left Ohio State with better numbers and a better understanding for how to flourish on the football field.

Woody was in attendance at the banquet, but Hubbard figured this would be the last time he would ever see his old coach, so he did not hold back.

"He was not afraid to speak his mind," said former Ohio State running back Archie Griffin. "He never has been. I think Coach Hayes respected that about Rudy."

Hubbard returned to Columbus to complete his physical education degree. A few weeks later, Woody called him to arrange a meeting. Hubbard assumed the cantankerous coach wanted to chide him for his heated remarks at the reception.

Not quite. Woody offered Hubbard the chance to become the first African American football coach at Ohio State.

"I was blown away," Hubbard said.

The Montreal Alouettes of the Canadian Football League had drafted the rights to Hubbard and had invited him to the Grey Cup. But by that juncture, Hubbard's interest in a professional career had waned, especially once knee injuries began to pile up. So, despite receiving a letter threatening his life if he took the job, Hubbard accepted Woody's offer.

Woody told his coaches that if everyone kept driving cars, there would be an energy crisis. So he typically walked to work. But by the time the team wrapped up with practice, Woody would be too exhausted to hoof it back home. He often called upon Hubbard for a ride. The two would stop for a pecan roll and hours of conversation.

"He dominated the conversation most of the time," Hubbard said. "Most people ended up doing whatever he wanted them to."

Hubbard challenged him at times, though. He fought for the responsibility of designing plays for the running backs. Hubbard played a role in recruiting Griffin to Ohio State and in urging Woody to include Griffin in the team's game plan. Griffin fumbled away the only carry of his first career game. A week later, he rushed for a school-record 239 yards against North Carolina.

"The reason I got in that North Carolina game is because [Hubbard] spoke up for me," Griffin said. "He had to skip over some other backs to put me in the game and in those situations, you better be right, because otherwise, you put your job on the line when you're dealing with Coach Hayes."

Woody helped Hubbard land the head coaching position at Florida A&M in 1974. Woody told him that if he worked his tail off, he could rescue any sputtering program and restore it to respectability in four years. Sure enough, in Hubbard's fourth season at the school in 1977, the Rattlers posted an 11–0 record. The following year, they went 12–1 and won the inaugural Division I-AA Championship. In 1979 they upset the University of Miami 16–13.

Hubbard coached at Florida A&M for 12 years, racking up 83 wins, the third-most in program history. He was inducted into the university's Athletics Hall of Fame in 1990. Woody died in 1987. Hubbard had two decades to ask Woody why he hired him on that winter day, after that frustration-fueled tirade at his high school. It is a regret that still haunts Hubbard years and years later. He wishes he had approached him about it, just to understand the coach's thought process, to understand whether Woody had identified something that signaled they could work well together or that they had a special bond. He could never build up the courage to confront the man, though. Many others who knew Woody can sympathize.

"We were all scared of Woody," Hubbard said. "I wasn't any different."

WE ARE MARSHALL

Ohio State hosted Marshall in the second week of the 2004 season, the first ever meeting between the Buckeyes and the Thundering Herd on the football field. The matchup took Keels back to his childhood.

Keels' mother worked at Xavier University, which afforded the family opportunities to watch the Musketeers play football before the school dropped the sport from its athletic arsenal after the 1973 season. Keels can recall one occasion in which Marshall topped Xavier in Cincinnati on a Saturday night at Corcoran Stadium on Victory Parkway.

Of course, many connect the Marshall football program to its tragic plane crash in 1970. It hit home for Keels for a couple of reasons. He saw those players perform on the football field at Xavier. As a 13-year-old, it was difficult for him to process. He struggled to come to grips with the gut-wrenching news. Three of the players who perished in the crash—lineman Mark Andrews, quarterback Bob Harris, and receiver Jack Repasy—had graduated from Moeller High School in Cincinnati, the same school Keels would attend the following year. In fact, the funeral service for the three players took place in the high school's gymnasium. The choir groups from the feeder-parish elementary schools participated in the service. That included Keels' parish. Keels was in attendance at the service with the boys choir from his grade school.

The memories came flooding back the week of the meeting between Marshall and Ohio State in Columbus in 2004. Ohio State ultimately slipped past Marshall in 2004 on a 55-yard field goal by kicker Mike Nugent as time expired.

Through a mutual acquaintance, Keels had been introduced to Mickey Jackson, once an assistant at Ohio State on Woody Hayes' coaching staff. Jackson also served on the staff at Marshall in 1970, but did not travel with the team on its fateful trip to East Carolina.

Jackson agreed to an interview with Keels the week of the 2004 matchup, and the two recalled the tragedy and its aftermath.

Jackson and Carl Kokor, another assistant coach, had been scouting Marshall's upcoming opponent, Ohio University. The Bobcats played that day at Penn State, so Jackson and Kokor were driving along the Pennsylvania Turnpike when they first heard the news of the plane crash that claimed 75 lives.

"We went straight to the football office, where there was quite a bit of confusion," Jackson said.

As the days passed after the crash, some "just wanted to roll up the tent and shut down the football program because of all of the pain," Jackson said. But, as documented in the 2006 film, *We Are Marshall*, an overwhelming outpouring of support and pride took over, especially once the NCAA opted to allow the program to bypass rules that mandated that freshmen were ineligible.

"[It took] unbelievable support from high school and college coaches to help rebuild the program," Jackson said.

Marshall basketball coach Dan D'Antoni provided a similar perspective during a pregame interview with Keels before the Thundering Herd and Buckeyes squared off in November 2016. D'Antoni noted how much of a setback and crushing blow it was to everyone at the university and in the athletic department, given the losses, which included key athletic department figures and boosters.

Marshall's first victory on the football field following the catastrophe came in 1971, a Week 2 win against Xavier in Huntington, West Virginia.

"It was unbelievable, so satisfying," Jackson said. "It was a sellout crowd, and I remember after showering and leaving the locker room, many of the people were still in the stands, with tears in their eyes."

CHAPTER 7
THE HEIGHT OF THE MATTA ERA

Evan Turner sat at midcourt, in a daze. A few teammates walked over to the junior swingman and offered to help him to his feet, but Turner refused all assistance. He opted to bypass postgame handshakes and headed directly to the locker room.

The reality of a hard-fought, season-ending loss did not take long to sink in for Turner. He didn't know it for sure, but he knew of the possibility. Everyone did. He might never again step onto the hardwood wearing scarlet and gray. The dream season had come to a crashing halt long before he had anticipated after a 76–73 loss to No. 6 seed Tennessee in the regional semifinals in front of a Rocky Top–shouting sea of Volunteers fans at the Edward Jones Dome in St. Louis. Ohio State, the No. 2 seed in the Midwest region in the 2010 NCAA Tournament, had greater aspirations than to fizzle out in the Sweet 16. And for Turner, a banner year full of hardware and historic accolades felt incomplete.

Turner, who finished with 31 points, had two looks at the basket in the closing seconds, as Tennessee clenched its three-point lead. Both shots fell short for the Big Ten Player of the Year and National Player of the Year. Turner felt as though he was bumped in the process. He thought he would be heading to the free-throw line for a chance at a three-point play. Instead, Ohio State was shut out.

"You want the ball in the hands of your best player," said guard Jon Diebler. "[Turner] is the best player in the country. We will live with having the ball in the best player's hands with 12 seconds left."

After the game, Turner professed what many elite college athletes do in the wake of a crushing defeat. He said there was no way he could go out like that, no way he could stomach his college career being capped by a frustrating letdown. Naturally, he reversed course two weeks later, when he announced at the Schottenstein Center his intention to enter the NBA Draft. He said it was the toughest decision he ever considered, and he wished he could have just disappeared. He had entertained the thought of leaving school early after his sophomore season, but he ultimately decided the only facet of college he wanted to escape early was his homework.

The Philadelphia 76ers selected him with the second overall pick in June 2010.

"I had the most fun I have ever had playing basketball," he said. "I think we grew as a team. We genuinely care for each other and have a lot of fun. To overcome the situations we had, we proved a lot of people wrong and just believed in each other—it was one of the best times in my life."

Turner turned in one of the greatest seasons in program history. He paced Ohio State in just about every statistical category imaginable: points, rebounds, assists, and steals per game. He owns two of the four triple-doubles in program history (Dennis Hopson and D'Angelo Russell recorded the others). He registered 16 double-doubles during the 2009–10 season. He was a consensus first-team All-American and was named Big Ten Player of the Week on seven occasions. And he delivered an unforgettable moment during the Big Ten Tournament (which Ohio State won), as he buried a buzzer-beating three-pointer from just inside the halfcourt line to knock out Michigan by a 69–68 final.

Here was Paul Keels' call:

"David Lighty will be the inbounder from the back baseline. Inbounds to Turner, left side of the backcourt. Turner across the timeline, throws it from behind high on the right—he hit it! He hit it! Evan Turner! He hit it just inside of halfcourt! Evan Turner, at the buzzer, knocks down a long three from high on the right! You gotta be kidding! Evan Turner hits a shot that everybody dreams of!"

As the ball dropped through the net, Turner kept his right arm raised, his hand pointing toward the floor. Diebler and Lighty converged to jump on him.

Ohio State's Evan Turner takes a last-second, game-winning three-pointer against Michigan, to give the Buckeyes a 69–68 victory in the quarterfinals of the Big Ten Tournament in Indianapolis on March 12, 2010.

Everything Turner touched that season turned to gold—at least, until the Sweet 16. Turner even fractured a pair of vertebrae in his spine while attempting a dunk in the first half of a game in early December. Doctors expected him to miss about eight weeks of action, but soon after, Turner said he would return to the court much earlier than initially anticipated. He ended up missing only a month of action, not nearly enough of an absence to derail his National Player of the Year campaign.

All the while, Turner had forged a close bond with his Ohio State teammates. It might not have been as talented of a team as the 2007 Final Four squad led by super freshmen Greg Oden and Mike Conley. But this was a tight-knit group aiming to return the program to that level of prosperity following a couple of ordinary seasons. Turner, Diebler, David Lighty, Dallas Lauderdale, and others would frequent Japanese steakhouses around Columbus. That was the team's tradition. And when they were not watching the chef create an onion volcano or juggle sharp knives, they would argue about whether Benihana or Genji was the premier restaurant. The group still reconvenes in Columbus each summer, even though players are now spread out across the globe.

"If food and restaurants are what we argue about, then I would say our friendship is pretty solid," Lauderdale said.

"It's funny," Matta said, "because, as I told them after the game, I wanted to be very careful with how I chose my words of what to say because, No. 1, I don't know if I have ever been more proud of a basketball team. And they had a belief about them that became contagious. And the quality of young men that we have on this team and just the togetherness that they had, I don't know if I have had too many teams that are close to this in regards to just who they were and their work ethic. Every day, they would come in and you just enjoyed being with them.

"They were never way up here. They were never way down here. They kind of just kept going. And I think that is the hardest part as you look at them after a game and they're distraught, because this isn't where they thought it was going to end. And when it comes to the point—we always talk about it as we start tournament play—it's one and done. You lose and you go home."

They came up short in March, but they had regained their footing as a program. Even with Turner's departure, the future was bright again for Ohio State men's basketball. The Buckeyes spent much of the following season as the top team in the country. They sprinted out of the gates with a 24-game winning streak that included wins against three ranked teams on the road: Florida, Illinois, and Minnesota. Ohio State entered the NCAA Tournament as Big Ten regular season and tournament champions with a 32–2 record, a résumé that merited the No. 1 overall seed for the big dance.

Matta warned his team about the danger of being a No. 1 seed. He was an assistant coach at Western Carolina in 1996, when the Catamounts nearly pulled off an unprecedented upset of No. 1 Purdue in the opening round of the NCAA Tournament. That team started its season 0–5 (and 3–10), including a two-point loss to Coker College, a private liberal arts school based in Hartsville, South Carolina.

"We started to mold together," Matta recalled. "We had some really, really good players on the team and upperclassmen. And, you know, going in, we felt like we had gotten what was conceivably the worst or the weakest of the top four seeds. And I remember when Kentucky [showed up on the screen]—they're the team that won it [that] year— our entire fan base cheered because we didn't have to play Kentucky. Those guys, they just had a unique way about them. They're probably the most innocent team I'd ever coached. Western Carolina had never been to the NCAA Tournament. And they were just sort of like, 'Hey, let's go out and have fun.' And they were a tough group of kids. They put themselves into a position to have a chance to win the game."

Western Carolina had a pair of looks on its last possession, but the team misfired on a go-ahead three-pointer and a game-tying mid-range jumper. No 16th seed had ever completed the feat until the University of Maryland–Baltimore County did the unthinkable and torched top-seeded Virginia by 20 points in 2018.

Matta shared with his players how, when he was with Western Carolina, they watched film of Purdue and thought there might be an opportunity to expose some of their weaknesses. The opposition certainly would not take the floor feeling like a massive underdog, so it was up to the Buckeyes to keep the foot on the gas pedal.

"He knows what it's like and what's going through [the other team's] mind," Lighty said. "So he was just telling us how we have to be focused and prepared and coming out ready to play."

Ohio State certainly did that. The Buckeyes breezed past Texas–San Antonio (75–46) and George Mason (98–66) in the first two rounds with scorching shooting at Quicken Loans Arena in downtown Cleveland. It was a homecoming for Lighty and Dallas Lauderdale, who grew up nearby. Matta recalled the countless drives he made up and down I-71 while recruiting the two. Ohio State fans filled the arena for the basketball weekend.

"To bring those guys home [for] the NCAA Tournament, I think it's very fitting," Matta said. "It's funny listening to them. They're all Cavs fans, and to have the opportunity to play in here—they have given so much to our program and they have given so much to the university that I'm excited for them to have that opportunity."

Before Ohio State's team shootaround prior to its Sunday matchup with George Mason, four seniors—Diebler, Lighty, Lauderdale, and Nikola Kecman—received their diplomas in an impromptu ceremony on the court in Cleveland.

"It definitely caught us by surprise," Diebler said. "It is something we didn't know was going to happen. It was a pleasant surprise. We didn't get to walk with our classmates. For them to take the time to do that and be thinking of us means a lot."

Miechelle Willis, a prominent member of the Ohio State athletic department staff, orchestrated the event. She called out the players' names, and they walked up, shook her hand, and took their diplomas.

"It was very special," Lauderdale said. "Graduating is very important to the Ohio State program. The music was playing in my head as I was shaking my classmates' hands, so it was fun."

Some eyebrows were raised when Kentucky was assigned a No. 4 seed for the tournament and placed in Ohio State's region. John Calipari's team blitzed its away to the SEC Tournament title and, though the Wildcats' top three scorers were all freshmen, they were mighty talented. Ohio State had a taller order than usual at that point in the tournament, as the two teams clashed in Newark in the regional semifinals.

In a closely contested affair, Diebler drained a three from the top of the key to tie the score with 21 seconds remaining. Kentucky's Brandon Knight nailed a pull-up jump shot over the outstretched arm of Aaron Craft to hand the Wildcats the advantage with five seconds to go. Craft fed William Buford for a clean attempt at a game-winning three at the buzzer, but the basketball clanked off the front of the rim.

That ended a season for Ohio State that seemed destined to have Final Four written all over it. There were coaching staff members who had family who were waiting to travel to Newark for the Elite Eight. There were Buckeyes fans I knew who were already checking out airfares for Houston, the site of the Final Four. Their plans were halted when a very successful season abruptly came to an end. That was one that kind of left you, like, "Wow, what happened here?"

Buford was Ohio State's second-leading scorer that season, with 14.4 points per game. He converted only two of his 16 field-goal attempts against Kentucky, though, unfortunate timing for a rare off-night. As a team, the Buckeyes shot only 33 percent from the floor, making 19 of 58 attempts.

Throughout the season, when Buford went on a scoring barrage or slipped up, Matta would shrug his shoulders and say, "Will's Will." Buford carved out a reputation as a goofy guy on the team. Ohio State had a road game earlier in the season against an opponent that many thought was superior. The day before the team departed Columbus, it gathered together to watch some film. Matta wrote on a marker board:

Airfare: $25,000
Hotel: $5,000
Food: $5,000
Miscellaneous: $4,000

Matta had one of the players add it all up. The total was $39,000.

"Fellas, if they are not picking us to win," Matta said to his team, "why wouldn't we just save Ohio State the $39,000 and we won't even go to the game?"

They all smiled and said they still wanted to go. Buford raised his hand.

"Coach," he said, "let me ask you: if we don't go, can we split the $39,000?"

Everyone in the room laughed.

"That's Will being Will," Matta said. "In terms of him as a player, it's been great to watch him grow and develop. I used to kid with him as a freshman [and say], 'If I were to stop the game in front of 19,000 people and walk out on the court and say, 'Will, what's the score and how much time is left?' he would have said, 'I have no idea, but I'm having the time of my life out here.'"

Buford returned for his senior season. Jared Sullinger came back for his sophomore year. The Buckeyes still had Craft and Deshaun Thomas. Even without Lighty and Diebler, Ohio State remained a threat to win the national championship. The Buckeyes finished tied for first in the Big Ten with a 13–5 conference record in 2012. They fell short against

Michigan State in the Big Ten Tournament final, but they earned a No. 2 seed in the tournament that mattered most. Matta's bunch knocked off Loyola (Maryland) and Gonzaga in front of plenty of scarlet-wearing fans in Pittsburgh in the first two rounds. They bounced Cincinnati and solved Syracuse's patented zone defense to advance to their first Final Four in five years.

For Sullinger, who could have been a first-round draft pick had he left school after his freshman year, it was a bit of validation. "I appreciated everyone that doubted this basketball team," Sullinger said, "said we were the underdogs, we weren't good enough, not mentally strong enough, not physically strong enough, mentally immature—we heard it all. When we were going through that slump in February, everybody was saying this basketball team was [going] downhill. We heard negative comments. I want to thank y'all, because through all of the adversity, we constantly pushed through that. I'm so proud of these guys. I mean, we came from nothing, according to y'all, to something now."

For Buford, the lone senior on the roster, it was a long time coming.

"It feels great," he said. "Nobody on this team has ever made it this far. In past years, I got to the Sweet 16. To make it this far is kind of a relief, to know that hard work pays off."

It might have been Matta's best coaching job, too, considering what Ohio State had lost from the previous season. Toward the end of February, the Buckeyes coughed up a late lead in a game against Wisconsin to suffer their third loss in a span of five games. Matta had kicked guys out of practice for a lackluster effort, and he thought the loss to the Badgers opened his players' eyes and made them realize that maybe they were not as good as they thought they were.

"That allowed us as a staff," Matta said, "to say, 'We have another gear. We can play better basketball. We can play more together. We can prepare better.' As hard as that loss was to take—having a lead down the stretch, we missed some free throws—maybe it got us pointed in the right direction. The thing I saw after that was when we weren't practicing well, guys knew it, and they could correct it. That's probably the No. 1 thing right there.

"This team is still so young, and you're still trying to learn what gets them going. I've kind of enjoyed that challenge, because they have been receptive to what we have asked them to do. I think they have an understanding of, 'Let's play for the team and good things will happen for me.' As we tell them all the time, the more you give of yourself, the more that's going to come back to you."

The Buckeyes were rewarded with a trip to the Final Four and a meeting with fellow No. 2 seed Kansas, anchored by big man Thomas Robinson, who averaged nearly 18 points and 12 rebounds per game. This was the situation Sullinger had envisioned when he opted to return for his sophomore season. Not only did he want to advance to the Final Four and vie for a national championship—he kept a poster of Knight on his bathroom mirror during the off-season as a means of motivation—but he missed Ohio State's early-season meeting with the Jayhawks because of injury.

"Me coming back was pretty much I wanted to make a statement," Sullinger said, "that not *everybody* is using college basketball as a pit stop to go to the next level. There is more than money and endorsements. There are championships that you get to win at every level. That's what I pride myself on. I've won a championship all the way from elementary to now. I pride myself on winning. That's the biggest thing. That's why I came back."

There was no storybook finish, though a Final Four appearance is nothing to sulk about. Kansas topped Ohio State 64–62 in a game in which the Jayhawks only led for 3:48. The Buckeyes led by as many as 13 points, but they shot only 34 percent from the field, including a combined 8-for-33 effort from Sullinger and Thomas. Kansas kept throwing double-teams at Sullinger.

"What you enjoy the most about coaching is the kids," Matta said. "What this basketball team has been able to accomplish, I'm extremely proud [of]. I didn't want the season to come to an end because I wanted to come back and watch film and go to practice and play another game with them. Watching these guys come together and all the great basketball they've played throughout the course of the season, all the great wins that they have been a part of, the whole locker room, they're special kids. That's probably the hardest part. By the same token, it's a tough job. It's a tough profession. I think you have to look at it and say, 'Hey, there are a lot of things we accomplished this year.'"

Matta seemed to push all of the right buttons with a relatively inexperienced team in 2012. The program was in a healthy place, even with the Final Four loss.

"There were so many unknowns," he said. "You had guys who did not understand how we wanted to practice. We did not understand the value of teamwork. At shootaround or practice [I was] reminding a player to tuck his shirt in. 'It has been 139 practices, please tuck your shirt in.' Those types of things. But I think that's the biggest thing we have tried to establish here in eight years is just the culture and environment for this program and how we want to do things. And I think that's where a lot of it comes from, the button-pushing, because there were so many unknowns with this team, and guys in their own minds thought, 'I'll be Jon Diebler. I'll be Dave Lighty.' But we didn't need them to be. We needed them to be themselves and play their best basketball."

CHAPTER 8

CARDALE'S COMING OF AGE AND SLAYING THE SEC DRAGON

One of Wisconsin's radio broadcasters approached Paul Keels at halftime of the 2014 Big Ten Championship Game at Lucas Oil Stadium in Indianapolis. "Well," he said, "what's your fourth-string quarterback look like?"

Following a Hollywood script—one that would be rejected for its impracticality—Cardale Jones directed Ohio State to a 59–0 thumping of the Badgers to capture the conference crown, one week after J.T. Barrett suffered a broken leg in the Big House in Ann Arbor, Michigan. Jones' magic didn't wear off after the Wisconsin win, either. The fairy tale persisted through the first ever College Football Playoff.

For a backup quarterback to come in and play three games like that for a national championship, that's TV material.

Well, technically, Jones was the backup to the backup. He committed under coach Jim Tressel, but the agreement included the condition that he spend a year at Fork Union Military Academy, a college prep school. Prior to that, he attended Ted Ginn Sr.'s Glenville High School in Cleveland. At Fork Union, which also jump-started the careers of Eddie George and Carlos Hyde, Jones roomed with receiver Michael Thomas.

The time at Fork Union—an all-boys program that permitted no TV or music, required early wake-up calls, and stressed studying and discipline—helped to mold Jones into a player mature enough to handle the spotlight and the challenge dropped into his lap at the end of the 2014 campaign. His first extended look came in the second half of Ohio State's 76–0 trouncing of Florida A&M in 2013. Kenny Guiton, filling in for an injured Braxton Miller, tossed six touchdown passes in the first half, earning him rest in the second stanza. Jones took over under center, but he did not attempt a single pass. With such a sizable advantage on the scoreboard, Ohio State ran the ball on every offensive snap in the second half.

Jones occasionally entered the huddle in spot duty throughout the rest of the season. He finished the year with one completion in two attempts, for three yards passing. The following year, Miller suffered a shoulder injury during practice in August, less than two weeks before the team's opener against Navy at M&T Bank Stadium in Baltimore. Miller's season ended before it even began. With Guiton no longer in the mix, Jones saw periodic playing time in relief of Barrett.

But no one could have seen this coming. Not the fan base. Not the coaching staff. Not even the 6'5", chubby-cheeked quarterback with the rocket arm and the reputation for valuing football over academics.

"He's a guy that, three years ago, was not equipped to handle this kind of situation," Urban Meyer said before the Sugar Bowl, Ohio State's first battle site in the inaugural College Football Playoff. "A year ago, he wasn't equipped. I started to see a gradual change. Tom Herman has done an excellent job with him. Spring practice, one day we walked off the field, and I was like, 'My God, he acts like a quarterback now. He's not acting like a child who's never been in a big arena.' And that's really a credit—we've all gone through it. Some go through it at age 55. Some go through it at age 15. And he's really matured."

In the two quarters before the Wisconsin radio announcer joked to Keels about Ohio State's quarterback hierarchy, Jones connected with Devin Smith on a pair of lengthy touchdown passes, Ezekiel Elliott rumbled for an 81-yard score, and the Buckeyes sprinted out to a 38–0 advantage. Jones and Smith hooked up again in the third quarter, and Ohio State treated the College Football Playoff committee to a nationally televised dismantling of the Big Ten West's elite.

All of a sudden, here comes this guy who had been around but hadn't really done a whole lot. He's thrown into a postseason situation with Wisconsin, where Ohio State needs to make a statement win, and all he does is go out there and play like he had been playing all along.

Ohio State quarterback Cardale Jones drops back to pass in his first collegiate start, the 2014 Big Ten Championship Game against Wisconsin, which the Buckeyes won 59–0.

Jones made a statement. Ohio State made the College Football Playoff. And a date with Alabama awaited.

The Buckeyes landed in Columbus at about 4:00 AM after the win over Wisconsin. Meyer fell asleep for a minute, but he quickly popped up, got out of bed, and went to work on the staff's recruiting schedule. He couldn't sleep, so he worked. (His family probably was not thrilled with this, since Meyer agreed when he accepted the head coaching position at Ohio State that he would strike a better balance between life and football. Working on recruiting schedules a couple hours before dawn likely qualified as a violation of that arrangement.) It irked Meyer that—while he obviously preferred that his team had a game—Big Ten Championship Game preparation would prevent the coaches from spending much time on the recruiting trail. Meyer called strength coach Mickey Marotti, who drove over to Meyer's house. The two sketched out two recruiting calendars: one for if the team qualified for the College Football Playoff, and one for if the team missed the cut.

The next day, athletic director Gene Smith joined Meyer at his house to watch the bowl selection show. Meyer was just as stressed about the team's playoff status as he was about his recruiting itinerary. This certainly was not the path many envisioned the Buckeyes would take, and not just because of Miller's health woes. Ohio State had lost to Virginia Tech at home in Week 2. The uphill climb Urban Meyer and company were already facing in August became even steeper starting in mid-September.

"I wasn't sure this year," Meyer said after the Big Ten title game. "I thought it might be next year that we would reach this, especially when we lost our quarterback."

Barrett, though, blossomed as the season progressed, with a 49–37 win at Michigan State in early November serving, perhaps, as the turning point on the schedule. In that game, Barrett threw for 300 yards, rushed for 86 more, and totaled five touchdowns. But as the Buckeyes topped Michigan in the final week of the regular season and Barrett lay on the grass at Michigan Stadium, the season seemed to crumble in front of everyone's eyes.

How was a program with, essentially, the third-string quarterback, going to do this?

If Ohio State had a chance against No. 1–ranked, perennial titan Alabama, it was because of the talent on the field that could ease the burden on the inexperienced quarterback. They needed Smith to serve as a lethal deep threat and Elliott to spearhead a potent rushing attack. They needed the defensive line to stuff the run and pressure the quarterback. They needed Jones to limit mistakes, avoid turnovers, and not fall victim to the blinding spotlight and media circus.

And then there was the coaching battle, a headline-grabbing duel between former SEC foes: Urban Meyer vs. Nick Saban.

Saban was wrapping up his second year as the defensive backs coach with the Houston Oilers in 1989 when he accepted the head coaching job with the University of Toledo. He hadn't devoted much time to preparing for his new role, as the Oilers went 9–7 and earned a playoff berth as a wild-card team. One day, a 25-year-old assistant coach at Illinois State named Urban Meyer called the Saban household. Saban's wife, Terry, answered the phone and spoke to Meyer. When Saban returned home later that night, Terry told her husband he ought to make a point to speak with Meyer when he assembled his new staff at Toledo.

"I was at Illinois State making $6,000 a year and making a decision either to stay in or out," Meyer said. "I was actually born in Toledo. I made a run [at it] and called his home. Had a great conversation. Nothing, obviously, materialized with it."

Saban was so fixated on the Oilers at the time that he never circled back to reach out to Meyer, who ended up taking a job as the Colorado State receivers coach under Earle Bruce.

"Obviously, that was a huge mistake on my part," Saban said.

"He said he regrets it," Meyer said. "I'm sure he does."

The two proceeded to find their way to the SEC, where they engaged in countless battles for conference championships and national title game berths. Meyer joked that he couldn't remember his address or phone number, but he could recall every play from the two clashes between his Florida squad and Saban's Alabama team, when the teams were ranked No. 1 and No. 2 in 2008 and 2009. In 2010, when Auburn and Oregon squared off for the crystal football, they worked together for a few days on ESPN's coverage.

When Ohio State and Alabama met on New Year's Day 2015, though, it was a bit of a David vs. Goliath proposition. Alabama had won the national championship in three of the previous five years, and the Crimson Tide entered as the top team in the country, the bastion of excellence in the conference that had captured the previous seven national titles and sent the Big Ten into a downward spiral.

"I know at some point," Meyer said, "if you're going to reach for the top, that you have to go through the top."

There was a lot of talk when Urban first got to Columbus about, "Would Ohio State become more like an SEC team and give Ohio State and the Big Ten a chance to compete for national championships?" When we knew they were going to play Alabama, that accelerated it even more. They had a few more weeks to work in Cardale to get him comfortable in being the starter, and Alabama had more opportunity to prepare for him, more than Wisconsin did. How would that all play out? Can they knock off the mighty Alabama Crimson Tide? I don't know if, that year, they were as loaded as they have been in some seasons since then, but they were still Alabama, still the team everybody thought would win the national championship.

"As coaches, we get such tunnel vision and locked into this singularity of purpose, you kind of lose sight of all the things that all these cameras are here for," said Ohio State offensive coordinator Tom Herman. "Maybe when it's over, and we come up for air and take a deep breath, the enormity of it might sink in a little bit more. But I think you kind of know it, but you just can't even think about anything other than your tunnel vision."

The day before the game, Meyer was asked how comfortable he was with his quarterback situation. Jones was the starter. Jalin Marshall, a receiver and punt returner, was—out of desperation and by process of elimination—the backup.

"Comfortable, not bad," Meyer said. "If you asked me a year ago or six months ago, I would have looked at you like you have six heads. But it's a much different story right now."

That was a nod to Jones' maturation and development. Meyer had some trust in the Cleveland kid. As Ohio State prepared for the Big Ten Championship Game, Marotti reminded Meyer that Jones had been in every meeting since Meyer and his staff took over a couple years earlier, that Jones understood the culture of the program and the expectations of the offense. That eased Meyer's mind a bit.

"The one thing that's not allowed," Meyer said, "is there are no excuses. It is what it is. So I feel very comfortable with where we're at."

The Crimson Tide opened up a 21–6 advantage midway through the second quarter. Alabama kept scoring touchdowns. Ohio State kept settling for field goals. But Elliott put his stamp on a 12-play, 71-yard drive with a three-yard score with just under three minutes remaining in the half. After an Alabama three-and-out, the Buckeyes struck again. In the waning seconds of the half, Evan Spencer corralled a pitch from Marshall, who had taken the handoff from Jones. Spencer stopped at the 22-yard line, halfway between the hashmarks, and delivered a spiral to Thomas, who completed an acrobatic catch by planting his left foot on the last bit of green grass on the far edge of the end zone before his momentum carried him toward a group of cameramen on the sideline. Ohio State had shaved Alabama's lead to one measly point at the half.

"Lou Holtz used to always say this when I worked for him," Meyer said. "When he first hired me at Notre Dame in 1996, he said—and I've always believed this, too—'The momentum, especially for a young team'—which, we're still a very young team—'is worth at least seven to 14 points during the course of a game.' And the most important momentum of any game is the last five minutes of the first half and first five minutes of the second half. We came out smoking in the second half, too, because I could hear it as we were walking in: 'We get the ball. We get the ball.' So we believe in that. I believe in it. And that's where, a lot of times, we're aggressive on both of those drives, because those are momentum-changing moments of a game, the last five and the first five."

Sure enough, Ohio State opened the second half with another touchdown drive. Jones hooked up with Smith on a 47-yard score to hand the lead to the Buckeyes. Steve Miller's 41-yard interception return tacked on another touchdown. Alabama closed the gap, but Elliott scampered 85 yards to the house to give Ohio State a 14-point lead with three minutes remaining. After the Crimson Tide struck again, many assumed the Buckeyes would attempt to run out the clock, especially given how effective Elliott had been on the ground. The sophomore had rushed for 220 yards in the Big Ten Championship Game, and he tallied 230 more against Alabama.

Instead, the Buckeyes ran the ball on only one of their three plays— and it was Curtis Samuel who carried the pigskin—and they promptly punted the ball back to Alabama.

"It was my call to throw it down the field," Meyer said. "You're not going to gain a yard anyways against very good players, [and] they were playing zero coverage. Everyone is within two yards of the line of scrimmage, and it was my call. So, maybe it wasn't the right call."

Alabama swiftly moved the ball into Ohio State territory.

"I just kept thinking I screwed this thing up," Meyer said.

But he knew he could rely on his defense.

"I have a lot of confidence in our defensive staff," Meyer said. "They have gotten so much better, our players, our defense, during the course of the season. So that's what all was going through my mind, was, 'Get that darn ball down so we get out of this with a win.'"

That is precisely what happened. Tyvis Powell picked off Blake Sims in the end zone and Meyer could relax. Elliott was named the game's Most Valuable Player for his rushing performance, which resulted from some extra motivation he was handed earlier in the day.

"Barry Sanders said before the game that there were two great running backs that were going to play tonight, and they both were for 'Bama," Elliott said. "I felt a little bit left out."

As for the program as a whole, it signaled a changing of the guard. Even though Ohio State still had a date with Oregon for the national title, the Buckeyes' upset marked the first time an SEC team—and, more specifically, the Alabama championship factory—had been humbled on such a grand stage in quite some time.

"We're back. We're back," said linebacker Darron Lee. "Those who thought we were gone—we're back. Be afraid. Be very afraid."

Hit the rewind button and take it back eight years. In the aftermath of Ohio State's championship game loss to Florida in January 2007, a friend—a devoted Buckeyes fan—dialed Keels' number. He knew Keels could not answer. After all, the head referee had just blown the final whistle. Meyer had just lifted the Crystal Football into the air. The Buckeyes had just sauntered back to the locker room, dazed and defeated, confused and conquered.

Still, he needed to talk to somebody. He needed to vent. Sure, Keels was still on the air, completing his broadcast from Glendale, Arizona, nearly 2,000 miles from Columbus. But a one-sided rant delivered to

Ohio State running back Ezekiel Elliott breaks free against Alabama in the 2015 College Football Playoff semifinal game at the Sugar Bowl in New Orleans.

Keels' voicemail would help to ease his conscience. Or maybe not. It would be worthwhile nonetheless. If it allowed him to feel one iota better about Florida's dismantling of No. 1–ranked, unbeaten, barely challenged, juggernaut emeritus Ohio State, it would be worth it.

He just needed to talk to somebody. I'm sure there were a lot of people who felt that way. It was one of those that, days, weeks, and months afterwards, it left you thinking, "Wow, that really did happen."

Entering November 2006, Tressel's squad had thrashed opponents by an average of 29 points per game, a run reminiscent to the one completed

149

by Woody Hayes' 1968 championship team, or by John Cooper's 1998 team (you know, until Michigan State turned Ohio State's world upside down). In November, they topped Illinois by seven, Northwestern by 44, and Michigan by three to earn a title game berth. And no one in their right mind—at least, no one north of the Sunshine State—considered Florida to be a threat to Ohio State's bid for an undefeated season.

And then: Florida 41, Ohio State 14.

There was nothing I detected that made me think they wouldn't show up on the field, throw the ball around, and win. You had the end of the season and then the whole buzz around Troy Smith winning the Heisman. I remember having to call a basketball game at Illinois and then getting to Phoenix just the day before the game. Even though we were staying at the same hotel, there wasn't anything that gave you a clue that Ohio State could lose. I remember reading about Florida being tired of hearing that they didn't belong and they played like they were tired of hearing that they didn't belong. That one was surprising, shocking, stunning.

Ohio State seemingly had everything going along so well on offense, defense, special teams. Troy winning the Heisman, it just seemed to be the setup for a real magical year. Here's Florida, who has to win their conference championship game to maybe get in. It was also very evident, after that Ted Ginn Jr. touchdown return to open the game, that Florida was the hungry team. They were the ones who felt like they had something to prove. It was early in that game when Tressel had the team go for it on fourth down in their own territory, something you wouldn't normally see Tressel do. That just showed the desperation of where they were. For a team that outmatched everybody throughout the course of the year, to see them outmatched, given that stage, that was incredibly shocking.

Tressel surmised that his team's exhaustive effort in the epic show-down against Michigan left the Buckeyes ill-equipped to handle the demands of a national title bout. He said Ohio State emptied its emotional gas tank a month too soon. By the time the Gators started to attack—after Ted Ginn Jr. was injured on a game-opening kickoff return for a touchdown—it was too late.

The seeds had been planted for the SEC's uprising and the Big Ten's nearly decade-long demise (which made it fitting when Meyer reversed the trends eight years later as the face of the Ohio State football program). It worsened a year later when a series of late-season upsets pitted Ohio State against LSU in the national title game. The Tigers, playing in their backyard at the Superdome in New Orleans, rolled to a 38–24 victory to send the Buckeyes to their second consecutive grand-stage loss to an SEC school.

"It's unbelievable to know you've failed two years in a row," said running back Beanie Wells, who opened the game with a 65-yard touchdown scamper on the fourth play from scrimmage.

As a method of motivation, Tressel had given his players a DVD containing 10 minutes of ramblings from talking heads from TV and radio outlets who slighted Ohio State's abilities. It did not work, and the Buckeyes were left to wonder how they could recover from a second straight January embarrassment.

Jonathan Wells, a running back for Ohio State from 1998 to 2001, is a native of Louisiana. For years, he debated his alma mater's merits with those living in SEC territory. "I argue all day with people I don't know on Facebook," Wells said. "I'm not going to tolerate any disrespect when you talk about the Buckeyes. I get it all the time—all of my LSU boys from high school. It doesn't help that they beat us in the national championship. At the end of the day, I'm still going to hold my ground."

The SEC dominance did not end after Florida and LSU washed their hands with Ohio State. Take a look at the list of college football champions from 2006 to 2012:

2006 **Florida**

2007 **LSU**

2008 **Florida**

2009 **Alabama**

2010 **Auburn**

2011 **Alabama**

2012 **Alabama**

Florida State topped Auburn for the 2013 title, but when Ohio State advanced to the first College Football Playoff a year later and Alabama stood in its path, it seemed as though another SEC beatdown of the Big Ten was on deck. Meyer even admitted to an awareness of a national perception that suggested Ohio State was not skilled enough to compete with Alabama.

"I think Lou Holtz was the only guy that picked Ohio State," Meyer said. "I think Robert Smith, maybe, but he's a Buckeye. There's a perception out here."

So how did Meyer train his troops to scoff at the notion that they were not good enough? It began with the other bowl games. "I think the tide turned a little bit when Wisconsin beat Auburn," Meyer said. "Everybody on our team knew that. I made sure they knew that."

Melvin Gordon rushed for 251 yards and three touchdowns, and the Badgers knocked off the Tigers in overtime by a 34–31 margin in the Outback Bowl. Later on New Year's Day, Michigan State erased a 20-point deficit in the fourth quarter to squeak by Baylor in the Cotton Bowl, 42–41. "We were pulling hard for [Michigan State]," Meyer said. "And our players—you should have seen their faces, man. They knew. They knew."

The coaching continued. They can do this. The SEC is not invincible. Alabama is not invincible. Meyer addressed the team at the pregame meal and delivered the message that reputation and conference allegiance did not matter. Ohio State had the talent, the speed, the athleticism, and the instincts to pull off the feat.

"Maybe the Big Ten's not that bad," Meyer said. "Maybe the Big Ten is pretty damned good. And it's certainly getting better. The mind is a fragile thing. You know, all of a sudden you get down against a team like [Alabama], that's No. 1 in recruiting every year for the past six or seven years. Our guys know that. You see them on film. Great team. But we're pretty good, too. And we went into East Lansing and beat a team that beat Baylor, and to play the way we did against Wisconsin, a team that just beat Auburn—that's the psychological approach to getting 18-, 19-, 20-year-olds to believe. We had a reflection moment with our team and a speaker the day before the [Sugar Bowl], and he talked about how strong belief can increase your level of play. Bad belief or poor belief can also lower your level of play. So there's no doubt that when we saw Wisconsin beat Auburn, that was a major, major moment for us getting ready for this game.

"The Big Ten…certainly showed that it is getting better. There's one way to silence people, and that's go out and play. We're a bunch of good coaches and players that worked our tails off and invested in a lot of resources into these traditionally great programs. So at some point you're going to get good results. I'm very fired up for our conference right now, because at some point, it gets exhausting when you keep hearing and hearing, and then you start believing. And that's fine if you coach, but if you're a player—pretty damned good players sitting [beside me]. They can play anywhere in the country."

Meyer considered the win against Wisconsin in the conference title game to be a breakthrough victory, since some of his veteran players would have otherwise left school without any degree of championship achievement. The Buckeyes finished with a 6–7 record during the transition year in 2011. The following year, they went 12–0 but were barred from postseason action. In 2013 Ohio State carried an unblemished record to Indianapolis for the Big Ten Championship Game, but they lost to Michigan State and then lost to Clemson in the Orange Bowl. So the win against Wisconsin in 2014 at least earned the seniors a ring. The win against Alabama—Meyer referred to it as "a sledgehammer game" and "a classic"—took them one step further.

"A guy like Mike Bennett, he's going to get a nice, big ring," Meyer said. "If he wins another [game], he gets a *really* big ring."

Meyer had grown tired of seeing the statistics about Ohio State's recent record against the SEC in bowl games (1–10, with the one victory, a Sugar Bowl win against Arkansas in January 2011, ultimately being vacated). "I just started seeing things flashing, flashing, kept seeing that stuff rolling through the TV the last week," Meyer said. "But it was a breakthrough win against an excellent team."

During Meyer's postgame press conference, the coach was asked whether the rest of the country was catching up to the SEC. "How much has the rest of the country closed the gap?" a reporter asked. "And, also, I think Oregon won by 40 today. Can you talk about—"

Meyer cut him off. "Oregon won by 40?" The coach looked as though he had seen a ghost.

The reporter said, "59 to 20."

"I gotta go," Meyer said, jokingly motioning as though he was about to sprint to the film room. "We gotta go get ready for that one."

"They put up that many points on a great Florida State defense," Jones said, "and they held that great offense to 20 points and caused so many turnovers from a team that's not known for that. I mean, it's been really impressive. When I heard the score at the end of the game, I was shocked. And then I watched the game, and I was even more shocked."

Shocked would also describe the reaction to Jones leading Ohio State past Alabama in the Sugar Bowl. In fact, Oregon quarterback Marcus Mariota, the Heisman Trophy winner, referred to Jones as a freshman.

"Well, of course, I'm not a freshman," Jones said.

That was not the worst he heard during his crazy month in the spotlight. "That I'm just back there, just playing backyard football," he said. "A lot of people think that we're just back there playing off pure talent, and they don't understand how much working goes into, really, each play."

The schedule made that preparation even more challenging. Ohio State had nearly a month to strategize for Alabama, but less than two weeks to gear up for Oregon (and recover from the exhausting Sugar Bowl victory).

"I want to make sure our players enjoy the journey," Meyer said. "These kids have been on a heck of a run for the last three years, and I'm more cautious about making sure it's not just an absolute grind. Someone asked a question one time, 'When does the joy of winning disappear and the fear of losing or the agony of losing overtake that?' When that does, that's not good. That's not good for anyone. So, I make sure that we enjoy the wins the best I can and the best our coaching staff can."

To go from all of the buildup to getting to New Orleans and seeing Alabama and the emotion involved in that, and then to turn it around and get ready to go to Dallas, it was, in some ways, like a regular season routine. It was crazy for us, getting all the stuff done that we need to, like pregame interviews and player interviews. I went a day ahead of our group so that I could be there for the media day and get interviews with players and coaches. It was a crazy turnaround.

It also meant another turn through the media gauntlet. The questions returned: Could a third-string quarterback really direct a team to a national title? Would Cinderella finally turn into a pumpkin at kickoff? Jones admitted that his confidence wavered as he sat back and watched Miller and then Barrett thrive on the field.

"It was very tough," he said, "being a No. 3 and then having two guys in front of you performing the way they were before Braxton and J.T. went down. It was tough to stay positive. It was tough to have that mindset, that I'm here for a reason. But with the help of my teammates and coaches, I got a chance to stick it out."

Jones won the backup quarterback job over Barrett in the spring, but Barrett reclaimed the top reserve standing during summer practice, before Miller was relegated to the sideline. Whereas other quarterbacks, stuck near the bottom of the depth chart, would transfer, Jones opted to stick it out in Columbus.

"The relationships I developed with not just our coaching staff, but our strength staff," Jones said, "and understanding the process—it wasn't like I was the best player as a freshman or I was the best player as soon as I walked on campus and I should be playing. I understood I wasn't that good. I understood there were things I needed to work on, and with the help of the coaching staff and the strength staff, I was hoping I could be at this point today.

"Being the third quarterback, coaches don't pay attention to guys really past the twos. I don't know of a situation [that] really happened like this, when a guy is playing, like a third-team quarterback, and just to keep that type of guy in line and being ready for this type of position just speaks to the coaching staff and the accountability that they hold on us."

For Jones, it clicked during that summer, when he realized he had a daughter on the way. Meyer noticed a change in him and told him, "Whatever it is, don't change. You're doing the right thing now, and you really have a future in this." About a month later, Jones told Meyer that his girlfriend was about three and a half months pregnant. Meyer did the math and realized that it was likely the impetus for Jones' maturation.

His daughter, Chloe, was born on November 7, the day before Ohio State's momentous win at Michigan State.

"Cardale has always had talent," Meyer said, "but really something happened in the last couple months. I know he had a little baby girl. Everybody in life has a chance to push restart. Not many people [get that chance] on a grand stage like Cardale has, and he pushed restart and he hit the right button, and that's called a selfless approach and a serious approach to how he handles his business, on and off the field. That's one of the great stories in college football and one of the great stories I've witnessed. I've told people, of all the things that my children learn in school, I want them to read about the case study of Cardale Jones, because it's a great one. It's a great one for everybody to read and learn from it. His maturity and growth are off the charts."

And so was his celebrity status. Seemingly overnight, Jones went from a guy known only to his teammates, family, and the most devoted Ohio State fans in Columbus to a national sensation. Receivers coach Zach Smith asked a few players to join him at the hospital because one of his cousins had undergone open-heart surgery. As Jones was leaving the hospital that night, a few nurses approached the quarterback and asked if he would surprise one of the doctors, who was a huge fan of his. Jones obliged, and the doctor started to cry.

"I'm like, 'Oh, snap,'" Jones said. "She said she was my biggest fan and stuff, so that was pretty weird to see someone cry because they got a chance to meet me."

In the days leading up to the playoff games, Jones blocked every contact in his phone except for his coaches and his mom. The process took him about 40 minutes. He even blocked his teammates, since he would be around them anyway. Jones wanted to eliminate all of the phone calls and text messages and friend requests. No distractions. Just football.

"I just want to put that much more into my preparation," he said.

Who could blame him? This was an opportunity few ever receive. For a third-string quarterback, it's usually a pipe dream. "This is unreal," Jones said. "This is like a freaking movie or a book. The best way I can describe [it] is basically just unreal. Every time someone asks me, I'm pinching myself. I can't pinch myself any harder, so I guess I won't wake up."

Of course, Jones still had to meet with the media. Reporters asked over and over how he was able to keep his composure in the unfamiliar spotlight, how he worked his way back into the good graces of the coaching staff and even about his relationship with his roommate, Powell, and their cooking exploits. "I'm going to try a taco salad," Jones joked. "We've got to get a fire extinguisher first in case anything goes bad."

Once it came time for the game, it was business as usual. No time for pinching himself or for browsing taco salad recipes. Jones played a mix of hip-hop for the bus ride from the hotel. Once he got to the stadium, he slowed things down, with John Legend and other R&B tunes.

Meyer had not had much experience with Oregon during his coaching career. When he was an assistant on Earle Bruce's staff at Colorado State, his team topped the Ducks 32–31 in the 1990 Freedom Bowl in Anaheim, California.

The stakes were a bit higher a quarter of a century later, and the Buckeyes rose to the occasion. Elliott continued his torrid rushing pace, with 246 yards on the ground and four touchdowns, including the final three scores of the game to put Oregon away for good. Jones accounted for a couple of touchdowns and 242 yards through the air in Ohio State's 42–20 win, and as the No. 4 seed playing with its third choice of quarterback, the Buckeyes emerged victorious in the first edition of the College Football Playoff.

Here's a guy who has an entire career in just three games.

Keels harkens back to the bus rides after the game and to the plane ride back to Columbus:

I just remember everybody seeming so tired. A long season, a long night, probably not a lot of sleep. Players, coaches, coaches' families and kids—there are a lot of people to get on that plane to come back. You would envision, at times, hooting and hollering and all of that stuff, but I think because there were so many people and it had been such a long stretch, it was quiet. The guy I remember who was really wound up, even that morning in the hotel before we left, was Kerry Coombs. I had known Kerry for a long time because of the Cincinnati connection. He was saying, "They can't really say anything bad about us now! They can't criticize us now!" He was being typical Kerry Coombs. But the day after the Oregon win, everybody was so tired. It was very subdued. I think everybody was just glad to get home.

There would be plenty of time to reflect on the team's accomplishments, to bask in the glory of an implausible championship run, to marvel at the way the Buckeyes dismissed the daunting odds staring them down and overcame each obstacle tossed their direction. There would be plenty of time for Jones to keep pinching himself, to keep wondering how this all came together in the perfect manner, at the perfect time.

"Long story short," Jones said, "we weren't supposed to be here. All the odds were stacked against us through the whole season, and for us to be sitting right here as national champs, it not only means a lot to me but to our community, Buckeye Nation, and our hometowns."

Even Meyer admitted that back in August or September, he did not think Ohio State had a chance to win a national championship. He thought the team could fight its way to some encouraging wins that would set the stage for a title run the following year. What a nice surprise.

"It seems like we've been through everything," Elliott said, "and it made us who we were."

Meyer's first team meeting with his new players three years earlier was also Jones' first day on campus. "The way he attacked the team and let us know it was time for a change," Jones said, "it started at the top with the culture."

The morning after the championship win against Oregon, Meyer and Jones had breakfast together. They reminisced about their journey together, about the unfathomable exclamation point the quarterback helped to place on the final sentence of a storybook script. A month earlier, Jones had not crossed anyone's mind. Now Meyer was being peppered with questions about whether Jones planned to declare for the NFL Draft.

"It's kind of cool to be sitting here using the word NFL next to Cardale's name," Meyer said. "I will tell you this: he could play in the NFL. He certainly has a talent. Is he ready right now? That's a chat I guess we'll go have at some point, probably not right here in front of everybody. You might enjoy that. But this is why we do what we do, to see guys [grow]. A theme that we have around our facility [is] it's never too late to change. Some guys change when they're 50 years old and it's too late. Other guys change when they're going through the journey like we all did when we're 17 to 21 years old, 22 years old in his case. Very proud of him."

They could not have done it without each other.

"The biggest thing with Coach Meyer," Elliott said, "is he just demands excellence out of everybody, every aspect of your life. When he demands that every day from you, you don't have a choice but to change."

Elliott looked over to Jones.

"You see," Elliott continued, "he had to change this clown, this goofball."

Troy Smith's Heisman-Worthy Maturation

Troy Smith arrived in Columbus as an athlete with little career direction. When Jim Tressel lured him to Ohio State, he did not promise Smith that he would play quarterback. He was, of course, all for Smith proving that he could.

Smith's five years at Ohio State were tumultuous at times and triumphant at others. Tressel was not thrilled with how the Glenville High School graduate handled his situation early on in his college career. "He didn't approach it the right way necessarily at first," Tressel said. "He let it really affect him through the beginning of his career."

Smith spent his first year at the school as a redshirt. He stood on the sideline and observed as the Buckeyes marched to a national championship in 2002. During his first season on the field, he primarily saw action as a kick returner and a scatback. He shifted to the role of backup quarterback to Justin Zwick the following year. When Zwick suffered a shoulder injury halfway through the schedule in a dreadful loss at Iowa, Smith took the reins.

The Buckeyes won four of five with Smith operating the offense, including a 37–21 beatdown of No. 7 Michigan at the Horseshoe. In that contest, Smith threw for 241 yards and two touchdowns and he rushed for another 145 yards and a score. Suddenly, the future appeared bright for Ohio State's offense.

And then Smith was suspended for the 2004 Alamo Bowl and the 2005 season opener against Miami (Ohio) for accepting $500 from a booster. The Buckeyes had no trouble with Oklahoma State in the bowl game or with the Redhawks in the early-September affair, but the uncertainty at the quarterback situation loomed large for the team's seismic matchup against Texas at Ohio Stadium in Week 2 of the 2005 season.

It was a battle between a pair of top-four teams, with the Longhorns ranked No. 2 in the nation and the Buckeyes slotted at No. 4.

In fact, Texas would ultimately win the national championship that season in a classic clash against USC in the Rose Bowl.

Zwick and Smith split time under center. Smith tossed a 36-yard touchdown to Santonio Holmes in the second quarter. Other than that, the Buckeyes only mustered field goals. Josh Huston accounted for five successful three-point kicks in all. Vince Young—who finished second in the Heisman Trophy balloting to USC running back Reggie Bush—connected with receiver Limas Sweed on a 24-yard score in the front left corner of the end zone with a little more than two minutes remaining. The Longhorns prevailed 25–22.

Smith eventually regained his starting spot and, after a hiccup against Penn State in State College, Pennsylvania, he never looked back. The Buckeyes rattled off seven consecutive wins to end the season, including a come-from-behind victory in Ann Arbor. Smith led a pair of touchdown drives in the latter stages of the fourth quarter to spur a 25–21 win against No. 17 Michigan. Six weeks later, No. 4 Ohio State topped No. 5 Notre Dame 34–20 in the Fiesta Bowl. Smith totaled 408 yards with his right arm and his legs, and threw a pair of touchdown passes.

"Your relationship with your head coach [and] assistant coach means a lot," Smith said after that win. "You are a coach on the field [as the quarterback]. Naturally, teams and people watch you, and the way you play on the field is pretty much a reflection of your coach, and everybody out there is pretty much cool, calm, and collected when we play, and that's the way Coach Tressel coaches."

That set the stage for Ohio State's bid for a national championship in 2006. The Buckeyes entered that season ranked as the top team in the country, and they maintained that standing until their fall from grace against Florida. Along the way, Smith became a no-brainer Heisman Trophy selection, Ohio State's first winner since Eddie George in 1995. At the award ceremony, Smith sported a dark three-piece suit with red pinstripes and a scarlet and gray tie. Even after he won, he said he was still in awe.

Ohio State quarterback Troy Smith looks to throw downfield against Penn State at the Horseshoe on September 23, 2006.

"Normally, I'm pretty cool in pressure situations, but my heart is pounding so fast now," he said. "I'm at a loss for words. I just can't believe this is happening. It means everything, just to be here in this situation."

All of Smith's early-career struggles had been placed in the rearview mirror.

"To watch him grow," Tressel said, "to understand, 'Okay, I know what it takes to be a quarterback, I know what I have to study, what I have to work on, what I have to be, what I have to get better at, and I know the type of leader I need to be—to see him five years later end up the Heisman Trophy winner when he didn't even come here to be a quarterback, or, he did, but we weren't sure—to me, that was very rewarding. Now, it wasn't without some consternation over the course of time, but it was fun to see at the end of the day.

"Those days that I see progress in each of the young people or a particular young person, you see a light bulb go on in someone's head or you see someone have a tough situation and then grow from it or handle it. My highlight would be progress."

CHAPTER 9
THAD MATTA

The question came the day before Ohio State's first game of the 2013 NCAA Tournament.

"What do you guys see behind the scenes that makes Thad so effective of a coach for you?"

A bit of a softball to open a press conference, sure, but Thad Matta had directed Ohio State's men's basketball program for nearly a decade. He had already guided two teams to the Final Four and had restored the reputation of a program that often lurks in the shadow of the football team, anyway. The Buckeyes were back in the big dance again, this time as a No. 2 seed and, again, backed by Final Four aspirations.

Aaron Craft hit leadoff.

"I think the biggest thing is Coach is one of the hardest workers that I have ever been around," Craft said, "and that really sets the tone for everyone else who's around him, whether it's watching extra film, whether it's getting in extra shots, just kind of being at the gym. That's who Coach is. He never wants to take any handouts. He wants to work for everything that he has gotten, and he has earned everything that he has been able to receive. He's just a great guy to be around. He's a players' coach. I can't say enough about him."

Deshaun Thomas took his turn next.

"He's a hard worker," Thomas said. "He's so competitive. I'm pretty sure he would be out there practicing with us if he could, showing us little moves or be out there diving on the floor. That's the great thing about him: He gets us ready and gets our minds right for any game and for watching film. He's always zoned in like we are. He's just like a player, like us, just so competitive and wanting to win."

It makes sense. Matta played, too, after all, at Butler University in the late 1980s. He cherishes one game in particular, in 1988, when his Bulldogs topped Dayton on the road and he nailed a game-winning shot in the final seconds. Here is how Matta remembers it:

We were down seven with, like, 1:56 to go. I was a sophomore then. Coach [Joe Sexson] calls a timeout and says, "We need some threes." So I come down and hit a three. We're down four. Stop them, come back down, hit another three. We're down one. We get a turnover with 20 seconds to go. Coach calls a timeout. "Here's what we're going to do. We're going to run this play and get the ball to [Chad] Tucker. If we can't get it to Tucker, get it to [Darren] Fowlkes. If we can't get it to Fowlkes, get it to [Jody] Littrell. If we can't get it to Littrell, get it to [John] Karaffa." And the horn goes off. "Wait a second, I'm in this game." I came down the court at the horn and threw it up. I scored about eight points the entire game. That's what type of player I was. That was the highlight of my playing at Butler University. Please don't make a big deal out of that. That's my one shining moment in college basketball. We can talk about my high school career. I was a better high school player.

That memorable game, of course, took place in Dayton, the site of Ohio State's first two NCAA Tournament contests in 2013, when Craft and Thomas were asked about what their coach brings to the table. The Buckeyes blew by Iona in the first round, but they required a last-second three-pointer from Craft to advance past Iowa State to another Sweet 16, the program's fourth in a row. Craft dribbled as the clock ticked down and, finally, when it became apparent that Ohio State had little brewing offensively, he launched the Buckeyes over the Cyclones. Craft wanted to feed Thomas, who fought through a pair of screens in an effort to get open. That didn't pan out. It didn't matter.

"I got their biggest guy on me, made a read," Craft said, "and, fortunately enough, it went in. I know if I wouldn't have made it, I think Deshaun was going to be a little angry at me for not throwing him the ball, so I think that gave it the extra oomph for it to go in."

Craft was never known for his shooting in his four years at Ohio State. He skinned his knees diving for loose balls. He gave opposing guards claustrophobia with his suffocating defense. He pestered the hell out of opposing coaches, who had to game-plan around him. So when Craft was asked, after his game-winning shot, if he ever practiced such a scenario in his backyard when he was a kid, he offered a fitting response: "I think we know I'm a defensive guy," Craft said. "So I think I was in the backyard, [going], 'Three, two, one...' and then taking a charge or something like that."

Craft remained the center of attention as the team advanced to Los Angeles for the next round. Craft was asked if he could see how someone might see him as annoying. Craft joked to Thomas that the reporter was actually asking about him.

"I know there are probably a couple people you could talk to back home that would say I'm pretty annoying outside of the basketball floor," Craft said. "But I think the way I play, I hope that's the way I'm viewed. That's what I try to do to other people, and I know in practice when Shannon [Scott] does it to me, I think he's pretty annoying as well. Anything I can do to make them think about other things and their game plan or anything like that, they can think as bad as they want about me, as long as they're not thinking about what they should be doing."

"I don't think he's annoying, really," Thomas added. "He doesn't guard me at practice or anything like that. He's on my team. So I like to see him get in peoples' heads, and other people think he's annoying. I don't think he's annoying, because he's on my squad and he's out there on the ball 90 percent of the time. So I like it. I can see he frustrates other point guards a little bit, because a lot of point guards like to force a lot of things. Especially scoring point guards trying to get their shots off and Aaron gets so into them. I think point guards see that, and I see it too."

Ohio State met Arizona at the Staples Center with an Elite Eight berth on the line. Just as they had in 2007, longtime friends and colleagues

Matta and Sean Miller would attempt to outmaneuver each other. When Miller contemplated moving on from Xavier in 2009, he reached out to Matta for advice. Matta stepped outside of the restaurant where he was dining to take Miller's call. They spoke for about an hour. When Matta walked back into the restaurant, his wife asked what Miller's final decision was going to be. "I have no idea," Matta told her. "I've never seen a guy jump from one side of the fence to the other as many times as he did."

Miller was intrigued by what Arizona had to offer, being one of the most prestigious programs on the West Coast and having been led by Hall of Famer Lute Olson for the previous quarter-century. Miller ultimately accepted the position, and the two buddies who coached together on Herb Sendek's staff at Miami (Ohio) in the mid-1990s were now in charge of two of the more respected programs in the country.

Matta recalled how, whenever the two of them went anywhere, Miller would forget his wallet. They were flying to south Florida one year to visit with Stan Van Gundy, who was serving as an assistant to Pat Riley at the time. Miller was on the coaching staff at North Carolina State. Matta was at Miami (Ohio). Miller set up the trip. They met at the airport, and Miller said, "You're not going to believe this. I forgot my wallet. You're going to have to pay for everything."

"He was making a lot more money than I was," Matta said. "But that's him."

The two shared an office for a year when they coached together at Miami. Matta said Miller was quite sloppy. Matta accepted a position on Butler's staff in 1997. The next day, Miller asked if Matta wanted to ride along with him to a basketball clinic, where Miller was scheduled to give a 10-minute speech at 8:00 AM. The two coaches did not know each other all that well at that point.

"We'll get in the car and come back," Miller said.

Matta asked where the clinic was being held. Miller said he was not quite sure, "but it's around here somewhere."

They left Oxford, Ohio, that night and arrived in Pigeon Forge, Tennessee, at about 3:00 the next morning.

"He got me," Matta said. "At that point, I kind of knew what I was in for. His personality, my personality, we've always gotten along really, really well."

When Miller left for a job on the staff at Pittsburgh in 1995, Matta reminded him that he owed him $350 for all of the lunches Matta had covered when Miller conveniently forgot his wallet. As Miller was leaving the office with a box full of his belongings, he told Matta, "Here's what I'm going to do. Call Adidas and you can have my money. I didn't spend it all, and it's cost-free."

"So he walks out the door, and I called Adidas," Matta said. "I said, 'This is Sean Miller.' They said, 'You no longer work at Miami University.' So he got me again. I've never been able to recover that money from him."

Miller joined Matta's staff when Matta became head coach at Xavier, and Miller succeeded him when Matta shifted north to Columbus. When they were both at Xavier, Miller would do a "trick of the day" at the end of their basketball camps. One time, Miller—a former point guard at Pittsburgh who was known for his ballhandling—offered $1,000 to any camper who could copy his moves.

"I'm like, 'Sean...'" Matta said. "And he said, 'Don't worry, they can't do this.' And he was right."

It's a good thing he was, because the odds were slim that he had his wallet on him that day, either.

Ohio State, the higher seed, was expected to defeat Arizona that evening in Los Angeles. "When you do this long enough, your paths are going to cross," Matta said. "I'm sure he feels the same way: I want to win like crazy, but if things don't go well, I couldn't be happier for him."

A bit of déjà vu unfolded at the Staples Center, as Craft again dribbled the ball at the top of the key in the waning moments with the score deadlocked. This time, Craft dished the basketball to LaQuinton Ross, who buried a go-ahead three-pointer with two seconds remaining. It was a fitting finish, considering Ross was using Kobe Bryant's locker.

Ross had been feeling good all weekend, though. During Ohio State's open practice the day before the Arizona game, he was talking to a teammate after nailing a few shots and joked that they should call over Reggie Miller—who was on the TV broadcast—for a shooting competition. After practice, Craft and Ross approached Miller, and Craft revealed what Ross had suggested. "I think I'm going to try to make him come out of retirement and shoot a little bit," Ross said.

The Buckeyes sputtered in the next round against Wichita State and fell short of a second consecutive Final Four ticket.

Still, that run of three years there had you thinking, "Okay, this thing can still keep going really well." Then, unfortunately, it dropped off. They lost the game in Buffalo to Dayton the next year [in their opening NCAA Tournament game], and that's when we started to see—for whatever reason—their recruiting wasn't as high and you also had some players who weren't as self-motivated. You think about what Evan Turner did, what David Lighty did, when those guys got there. They not only benefitted from coaching, but they were also self-motivated and worked hard at improving their game. They brought in all that talent in Greg Oden and Mike Conley, but Turner and Lighty are probably the two best examples of guys who made themselves into better players. Unfortunately, we didn't see that at the end of Thad's time, guys who made themselves a whole lot better.

Dayton, the No. 11 seed in the south region, slipped past No. 6 seed Ohio State 60–59 in 2014. A No. 10 seed the following year, the Buckeyes bowed out against Miller and his Arizona squad before they could notch another Sweet 16 appearance. The two seasons after that sealed Matta's fate. Ohio State missed the tournament in back-to-back years for the first time under Matta's leadership. The Buckeyes mustered a 17–15 mark in 2016–17, including a 7–11 record in Big Ten play, their worst conference showing since Jim O'Brien's last season at the helm. Some players were injured. Other players had transferred. The program's recruiting had declined a bit. Matta's health had become an issue, as he had battled back issues for a long time. There was one year in which he could barely walk. After games, back pain made it difficult for him to take off his shoes and his pants. He would have to gear up just to address the media after games. Coaches at other schools eventually started to use Matta's health as a negative recruiting tactic. They would convey a level a risk to players who were considering Ohio State.

"Maybe to a fault, I always fought," he said. "I felt I had to do that for the players."

In June 2017, Ohio State scheduled an early-afternoon press conference, which sparked speculation about the direction of the program and Matta's job security. A few days earlier, Matta and athletic director Gene Smith had decided upon a split. The winningest coach in program history was out of a job after 13 years, which Matta referred to as the greatest 13 years of his life.

Matta quoted the Grateful Dead song, "Truckin'," during the press conference. "If you wanted an exact thought of where my emotions are," he said, "there's a great song that says, 'Sometimes the light's all shinin' on me / Other times, I can barely see / Lately, it occurs to me / What a long, strange trip it's been.'"

Matta wrapped up his Ohio State tenure with a 337–123 record, five Big Ten regular season titles, four Big Ten Tournament titles, and two Final Four appearances.

"I hope, No. 1, I'm remembered as a really good person," Matta said, "a guy who cared about the university, a guy who cared about his players. I think, from that perspective, that is probably what is most important

Former Ohio State head basketball coach Thad Matta watches his team during practice before the Buckeyes' Final Four appearance against Kansas in March 2012 in New Orleans.

to me. You know, the wins, the losses, those things, they come. We had a stretch here that was probably about a five-year stretch as good as anybody in the country had, in terms of college basketball. I think the last thing I hope I'm always remembered for is that we always did it the right way. That, to me, is something I'm going to hang my hat on, that this program was run the right way."

Matta joked that if he ever coached again, it would be in track and field, not in basketball. "When the parents want to cuss me out after the game," he said, "I can say, 'This is the time your son ran. I can't help you on that. There were no shots, no touches, anything like that.'"

It was an ending that, obviously, was not easy for any party involved: coach, university, players, or fans. And once again, Ohio State was faced with searching for a new head coach late into the basketball off-season.

A few days after the press conference, Ohio State introduced Chris Holtmann as its new head coach. Holtmann had to postpone a vacation to Hilton Head, South Carolina, to sign his contract in Columbus, a small consolation for his move from Butler to Ohio State. Holtmann ensured the players that it would not be a transition year, and he wasn't kidding. The Buckeyes, picked by the media before the season to finish 11th in the conference, actually finished second, with a 15–3 record.

No one really knew what the Buckeyes had on their roster, though. Kaleb Wesson followed through on his commitment to Ohio State, even though he had originally done so under Matta. Kyle Young relocated from Butler to Ohio State. Marc Loving, JaQuan Lyle, and Trevor Thompson had all moved on in one way or another. Keita Bates-Diop was returning to the lineup after a medical redshirt season, the result of his suffering a stress fracture in his leg.

Andrew Dakich had been a reserve at Michigan and graduated with one year of eligibility remaining. He was pursuing his options as a graduate transfer and initially landed at Quinnipiac University in Connecticut, but he encountered some academic scheduling issues. Dakich's father, Dan, a former player and coach at Indiana and broadcaster for ESPN, relayed his son's predicament to Holtmann. Ultimately, Dakich wound up in Columbus.

This was not the first case of a Michigan man venturing south to enemy territory. Columbus native Justin Boren fled the Wolverines for Ohio State under Jim Tressel. His younger brothers, Zach and Jacoby, eventually followed suit and attended Ohio State. The Boren brothers' parents actually had attended Michigan.

There were unknown commodities. We were all in for a surprise. As practice began, I can recall attending an early session in which Holtmann mentioned they were trying to introduce things in a simple manner and not overload early with specific plays. What was apparent was this team was going to go as far as its two returning leaders, Jae'Sean Tate and Keita Bates-Diop, would take them.

The Buckeyes stood at 5–3, with losses to Gonzaga, Holtmann's old Butler bunch, and Clemson. They trekked north to Madison for a matchup with Wisconsin on December 2, the same day the two schools' football programs met in Indianapolis for the Big Ten Championship Game. The Buckeyes emerged victorious in both contests, and their 25-point drubbing of the Badgers set the wheels in motion for a more prosperous season than anyone had envisioned. Ohio State started 9–0 in conference play, including a win against Michigan State, ranked No. 1 in the country at the time. In early February, as the Buckeyes were climbing up the national polls, they knocked off No. 3 Purdue in West Lafayette, as Bates-Diop converted a follow-up shot in the closing seconds for a 64–63 triumph.

Ohio State earned a No. 5 seed and a date with No. 12 seed South Dakota State at Taco Bell Arena in Boise, Idaho, where Keels had called his last hoops game for the University of Cincinnati 20 years earlier. The charter flight to Boise included not only players and coaches, but also family members of coaches and staff members. A vast majority of those on the plane were visiting Boise for the first time. While a player at Taylor University in the early 1990s, Holtmann had participated in a tournament in Nampa, Idaho, about 20 miles west of Boise.

"I knew you guys were known for potatoes and pretty much just [Boise State's] blue field," Tate said. "And once I got off the plane, I was expecting it to be a little colder, but it was way more beautiful than Ohio. It was warm. And just the view of the mountains and that—I didn't expect having that coming off the plane."

"I kind of liked the mountains," said Bates-Diop, the Big Ten Player of the Year. "We don't have that in Ohio. To see mountains coming off the plane, that was pretty nice."

The Buckeyes avoided an upset against the Jackrabbits in the opening round. They nearly knocked off Gonzaga two days later, but the Bulldogs bested the Buckeyes for the second time in four months. When the game ended, the coaching staff thanked the players for the valiant season rather than discuss where they erred against Gonzaga.

The unexpected ride for the Ohio State basketball team ended in a place that would have been very hard to foresee prior to the start of the season. This team provided all who paid attention with exciting moments and a hope for more to come. We once again had a chance to see that, while understandably, football drives the bus for this university's athletic department, when hoops are hot, the winter cold is much easier to deal with.

Covering Thad Matta

by Paul Keels

Paul wrote this essay in the days after Thad Matta's dismissal from Ohio State in June 2017. He never shared the piece with anyone until it came time to piece together the chapters of this book.

Whenever radio announcers who broadcast games for college teams get together, the topic of dealing with the coaches you cover almost always comes up. For most of the '90s, when I was doing games for the University of Cincinnati, people thought I had a burden working with Bearcats basketball coach Bob Huggins, and it couldn't have been further from the truth. Bob was a guy who was brutally honest in radio interviews, often gave you more info than you expected, and appreciated an interviewer who did his or her homework.

While I truly thought working with Huggs was a great ride, it was surpassed with the guy I dealt with for the last 13 years: Thad Matta.

In 2004 Matta came to Ohio State after three successful seasons at Xavier (ironically, where I went to college) and took over the Buckeyes' basketball program at a difficult time. Jim O'Brien had been a very popular coach who made Ohio State basketball relevant again. His second Buckeyes team in 1998–99 shocked the world, rebounding from a 22-loss season the previous year and making the Final Four, the first at Ohio State since 1968. Sadly, things would come to an unfortunate end, with Jim being dismissed, and that Final Four and many other games were vacated due to rules violations.

Matta took over players he did not recruit and campaigned with incoming players who had signed letters of intent for another coach (one of whom, Je'Kel Foster, he had never seen). But in doing so, he brought an optimistic attitude not uncommon for coaches at new places, but an attitude that told us who he really was.

That first year, guys who had underachieved in previous seasons showed new spunk, and their play fit the optimism of a new voice, both from the head coach and the coaching staff. The crowning moment for a team that was saddled with a postseason ban was defeating No. 1–ranked and undefeated Illinois in the final regular season game of the year. It was the same Illinois team that was dancing on top of the scorer's table the previous season when they clinched the Big Ten title on the Buckeyes' floor.

From there, good things were to come for Coach Matta and his band of Buckeyes: Big Ten titles, Final Fours, a national title game appearance. But during all of this success, Thad was the same guy he was when he first hit campus. I have a feeling he was the same guy who first got started as an assistant coach at Indiana State under Tates Locke. He was always good about pregame and postgame interviews, weekly radio shows, countless daily interviews. Most importantly, during the times of great success, when the networks were all craving his time, he still made the time for his local radio guys. Also, just as importantly, after tough losses—and the last two years, which were difficult seasons—he was still there when his radio obligations required him to be (excluding any times in which logistics or postseason tournament limitations prevented him).

It's important to add that not only was he always available, he was also very forthcoming, entertaining, and informative in the times I dealt with him as a radio announcer. He was very respectful of not only us, but to the listening audience as well.

There has always been that unwritten warning about becoming friends with coaches you cover. Dealing with Thad Matta was the exception to that. Like most coaches, he could tell stories with the best of them. But he also welcomed stories from others, took interest in our lives, and included a select few of us into events with his family. Being around his wife, Barbara, his daughters, Ali and Emily, as well as his parents and in-laws was also a wonderful part of the experience.

Almost all coaches talk about how, most likely, their time will end, and not by their own choosing. It's a sad but true fact of the profession, it would seem. While Thad Matta's chapter as coach at Ohio

178

State has ended, many of us are better for the time spent with him, his coaches, and his family. His records and accomplishments speak for themselves. We have seen the tons of tributes from his former players. Any Buckeyes fan who has been fortunate to get time with Thad will have a connection for which hopefully he or she will be grateful.

Rest assured, there is one radio announcer whose experiences have been made memorable because of the coach he got to cover for 13 years.

CHAPTER 10
KEELS' FAVORITE PLAYERS

Over the last 20 years, Paul Keels has developed a rapport with a litany of football and basketball players. He has interviewed some during the season. Some have joined him on his weekly radio show. Others have worked at the radio station following their college football careers. The following is a rundown of memories Keels has about some of the names that stand out the most, starting with the football players.

Michael Wiley (RB)

One of the first Ohio State players I had the chance to interview, Michael's senior season provided quite a few highlights, as well as interview opportunities. He was seemingly always upbeat and a good interview. Once his professional career was over—he spent three seasons in the Dallas Cowboys' backfield—he returned to Columbus, and I have had the chance to run into him on numerous occasions. He is always as welcoming as when he was a player.

Matt Keller (FB)

This was one of the earliest interviews I sought out, because we both graduated from Moeller High School in Cincinnati. That was a door-opener that made for at-ease interviews, and I even learned that we shared connections to the same grade school parish. I ran into him in later years in Cincinnati.

Dee Miller (WR)

While Dee was part of an outstanding receiving corps in the late '90s at Ohio State, my contact with him came after both his college and professional football days came to a close. Having returned to Columbus and become an insurance agent, Dee is someone I get to see fairly regularly. He has become an on-air performer for some of our Ohio State–related radio shows, and it's always interesting to hear him talk, not only about his playing days, but his views on the present-day Buckeyes.

Jerry Rudzinski (LB)

Another of the very first group of Ohio State players I had the chance to interview, Jerry was one of those guys who seemed to be a go-to player for much of the media. He was one of those guys who was easy to root for when he played, and it was great to see him score a touchdown on a fumble recovery during his senior year. Jerry is another former player who has become involved with our radio station's football programming, and it's always great to see him and ask about his wife and five children.

Rodney Bailey (DL)

Rodney was another one of those players during the John Cooper era who was always a good interview and who showed a warm personality, even as a college player. After his lengthy professional career—he played for the Steelers, Patriots, Seahawks, and Cardinals—I have had a number of chances to run into him, and in one of the most recent occasions, he presented me and others with autographed copies of his snapshot in the White House with the Super Bowl trophy from his New England Patriots days. That picture hangs in my cubicle at work.

Gary Berry (DB)

Always a willing interview subject, I recall Gary scoring a defensive touchdown at Michigan State. He is one of those guys you don't see very often, but when you do, it makes you feel better for running into him. I had the chance to meet his mother on a handful of occasions during basketball games when his sister was playing at Purdue.

Steve Bellisari (QB)

As you could imagine, the starting quarterback at Ohio State would always get a ton of media attention, but Steve was one of those guys who, during interviews, seemed to have recognition of those people who were around on a regular basis. He was also someone who, for some reason,

I just happened to bump into from time to time outside of those interview sessions, and he was always just as congenial at those times as he was when there were hundreds of microphones pointed at his face. It also made for a good finish to watch him end his career at Ohio State with a career-best performance in his last game, even though it came in a three-point loss to South Carolina in the Outback Bowl.

B.J. Sander (P)

Again, there is a hometown connection here. Since B.J. was also from Cincinnati, that provided a jump start when meeting him at first and getting the chance to interview him. He seemed to warm to that connection, and we had a few chances to just chit-chat about Cincinnati stuff. It was an enjoyable experience to witness the season in which B.J. won the Ray Guy Award for being the nation's top punter.

Mike Nugent (PK)

It should be pointed out that during the Jim Tressel coaching tenure in Columbus, there were times when the pickings were slim during media availability. At times, the kickers and punters would be all we had to work with. Mike was among the most well-spoken of all of the players during his time as a Buckeye, and that was helped by the tremendous success he had while playing at Ohio State. (In the interest of full disclosure, Mike became one of my favorite players because he revealed that he was reading my previous book, *Tales from the Buckeyes' 2002 Championship Season*, for one of his classes.) During broadcasts, we still, on occasion, make reference to his game-winning, 55-yard field goal in the closing seconds of a win over Marshall at Ohio Stadium in September 2004.

Craig Krenzel (QB)

When thinking about Craig, the first thing that comes to mind is how in his first start in 2001, he helped Ohio State pull off a major upset in

Ann Arbor against Michigan. The Michigan native would then go on to quarterback the 2002 national championship team. But most of my real connection with Craig came after his college and professional days were over and he became involved with some of the shows at our radio station. Known for being the trigger man on some of the most crucial, celebrated plays during that championship season, my dealings with Craig now involve him handling my home and auto insurance.

Ohio State quarterback Craig Krenzel looks to pass during the Buckeyes' 50–7 defeat of San Jose State in October 2002 at Ohio Stadium.

Mike Doss (S)

He was known for such hard hits coming out of the defensive secondary that often times, when he made plays at Ohio State, we would reference them by saying, "Sounds like Doss!" He is also remembered for making a public and emotional announcement about staying in college for his senior year, rather than turning pro, in hopes of winning a national title. How prophetic! Mike was always a media favorite, and he even joined us on the air once while playing for the Indianapolis Colts during an Ohio State bowl game. He discussed how the Colts players rallied around then-coach Tony Dungy following the death of his son. Mike is another Buckeye who has settled in Columbus after his playing days, and it's always a good experience to shake his hand.

Dustin Fox (S)

Knowing he came from a family with a broadcasting background, it stood to reason that Dustin would be a favorite for all who covered Ohio State. It was his friendly personality that added to what we all experienced in being around the young man. It's no surprise that he caught the broadcasting bug once his playing career ended. Dustin ranks very high on my list, as he also reached out to express concern when I missed a pair of games during the 2010 season because of an unplanned surgery.

Brandon Joe (RB)

A Columbus native who spent most of his time as a blocking back for others who carried the ball, Brandon displayed an engaging personality along with a delivery and a voice that could have placed him in the media industry, but he chose a different path. I can recall an interview I conducted with Brandon in which one of his backfield mates, Maurice Hall, boasted that, with his personality, Brandon could one day be mayor of Columbus. He's one of those guys who, post-football, is a joy to run into. With his unselfish play on the field, it was great to see him get a chance in one game to rush the ball quite a bit and even find the end zone in Ohio State's 2004 victory against Penn State.

Matt Wilhelm (LB)

Not only was Matt memorable for his play as starting middle linebacker for the 2002 national champions, but he was as well spoken as any Ohio

State player who was made available to the media for interviews. The night before the national title game against Miami, Matt and defensive lineman Tim Anderson were watching film, and they allowed me to enter the room so I could tape a pregame interview. It was no surprise that after Matt's NFL career concluded, he shifted into the broadcasting profession. While I have been flattered to appear as a guest on Matt's shows, it was an even more enjoyable experience to have him fill in as our sideline reporter for the Ohio State–Michigan game in Ann Arbor in 2017.

Tim Anderson (DL)

After his playing days, Tim returned to Columbus, and I had a chance to run into him a handful of times. He was just as pleasant on those occasions as he was that championship eve back in 2002 in Phoenix. I also have a fond memory of Tim grabbing an interception in Ann Arbor against Michigan in 2001. It was notable because you don't see defensive linemen come up with interceptions very often.

Mike Kudla (DL)

The first thought that comes to mind when thinking of Mike Kudla is him falling on a fumble in the north end zone in the fourth quarter at Ohio Stadium to help the Buckeyes score an overtime win against Purdue in November 2003. A highly sought-after recruit and a guy who made plays on the field that demonstrated his incredible physical strength, Mike was one of those players who made you feel like he was really paying attention to what you were asking him. He was very polite and respectful and understanding that you were doing a job.

Malcolm Jenkins (DB)

People have become more aware of Malcolm because of his on- and off-the-field presence in the NFL, but he was just as impressive of an individual while at Ohio State. Interviews with Malcolm were opportunities to talk with an intelligent and classy person who you just knew was destined for good things with the sport. Plus, it was apparent how he could influence things more important than football. Seeing him flourish on the football field seems like just an appetizer for what may come for Malcolm, and we should all look forward to what he may achieve in the future.

Troy Smith (QB)

When Troy finally took over as starting quarterback, you noticed not only his special skills, but how he could affect those on the field with him and his leadership of the Buckeyes' offense. Troy, at first, was not a great interview, but he eventually became "Tresselized," ultimately sounding much like his head coach. He developed into a smooth talker and often referenced the ability of his offensive linemen. Troy's Heisman Trophy–winning season was incredible to witness, and his touchdown pass to Brian Robiskie against Penn State—which included him eluding defenders who seemed to have him surrounded—was a moment that may have jump-started his campaign.

Nate Salley (DB)

Nate played both football and basketball while at Ohio State, and my familiarity with him came more from the hardwood. When head coach Jim O'Brien needed an extra body, Nate heeded the call, knowing his chances to get on the court were better in practice than in games. It was during the hoops season that I had the chance to be around him more, which in turn led to a stronger rapport for interviews during football season. As polite as any Buckeye, Nate always seemed to light up when it was mentioned that he was a two-sport athlete.

Antonio Smith (DB)

A young man who achieved academic success, Antonio waited patiently for his chance on the field and, as a senior, became an all-conference performer. He took polite to a new level, as he was always a pleasure to interview and to speak with. He was easy to root for, especially when he received all-league honors, and he even scored a defensive touchdown on a 55-yard interception return against Penn State in 2006—a little more than one minute after Malcolm Jenkins completed a pick-six of his own. Antonio is one of the classiest players to ever wear an Ohio State uniform.

Kirk Barton (OL)

Always a go-to player when in need of an interview subject, Kirk ranks high because he enjoyed the conversations and had aspirations of getting into the media industry. He was always a guy who enjoyed the interaction with the press, and that continued as he worked as a graduate assistant on Jim Tressel's staff. Kirk is blessed with an outgoing personality, and I still think he would make a good sports talk show host.

Orhian Johnson (DB)

I got to know this young man from St. Petersburg, Florida, because I was often assigned to sit next to him on the team's charter flights. I was impressed with his demeanor, and he also took particular concern when I had to miss the road game at Wisconsin in 2010 because of my surgery. When I had the chance to see Orhian outside of football events, he was just as pleasant as he had always been.

Marcus Freeman (LB)

A soft-spoken but very engaging young man who blossomed into a quality football player, Marcus was among the most polite players to interview. He seemed to have a knack—at least, in my case—of remembering who you were, and that made being in his presence a pleasant experience. While health concerns cut short Marcus' professional playing days, it has been great to see him experience success as an assistant coach in the college ranks.

Evan Spencer (WR)

Evan merits mention here in part because of his parents, Gilda and Tim. His dad was an assistant coach at Ohio State under both John Cooper and Jim Tressel, and he was a teammate of my broadcast partner, Jim Lachey. Evan, however, was also an impressive interview, and it was fascinating to watch his playing career develop. For many, Evan will always be remembered for throwing a touchdown pass on a reverse against Alabama in the College Football Playoff semifinal. Later that night, after the game, I saw Gilda, who was excited about the play but also relieved that it proved to be successful.

Joshua Perry (LB)

Anyone who has ever met this young man will understand why he stands out—not just because of his God-given physical attributes, but for his entire presence. Joshua is well-spoken, gracious, polite, humble, and exactly what I would think any parent would want their son to be. Not to mention he was also an incredibly talented player who continues to excel at the professional level.

Billy Price (C)

Some offensive linemen enjoy being interviewed because they don't often receive the recognition that other position groups attract. Billy, early on, became one of my favorites because he was quite conversational, upfront, and informative, and he always discussed things in a team-oriented manner. On the rare occasion that a game did not go well, Billy was one of those who was always willing to talk when it was not the ideal postgame activity. He was easy to root for, and that will continue as he plays at the next level.

Parris Campbell (H-back)

A young man with a magnetic smile and a warm personality that is revealed from the get-go, Parris enjoys playing football, enjoys talking about it, and enjoys being a football fan. His skills are impressive, and he seemingly still has room to grow, based on what the coaches say. The handful of times we have interviewed him have made for good programming.

Sam Hubbard (DE)
Sam and I share a high school alma mater. A player who had rave reviews attached to him during his redshirt season, it was exciting to see Sam burst onto the scene and demonstrate his playmaking ability. He's an extremely polite young man who provided great interview material. It was great to run into him, shake his hand, and wish him the best at the next level.

J.T. Barrett (QB)
The story of his career in Columbus and the records he set as a Buckeye will loom large as part of his legacy, but for all of the things J.T. accomplished on the field, he was as impressive to those of us who had the chance to interview and get to know him. He was classy, well-spoken, teammate-oriented, and competitive. J.T. delivered countless memorable plays and moments. During his senior year, he was always in demand by the media, and it was highly appreciated how cordial he was.

There are other players who I did not have much exposure to during their Ohio State careers, but who I came to know in other capacities during their post-football days. Linebacker Bobby Carpenter now cohosts a talk show at our radio station, and on occasion, I get the chance to reminisce about his playing days, the coaches who molded him, and his outlook on the current Buckeyes. The same goes for running back Beanie Wells. I have crossed paths with others, such as linebackers James Laurinaitis and A.J. Hawk, at various events. Both have dipped their toes in the broadcasting waters. Quarterback Bobby Hoying has been very welcoming when I've run into him. Quarterback Jim Karsatos, who was part of our broadcasts for years, has become a friend with whom I have shared many great experiences, such as the 2002 national championship. I'd also like to include defensive back William White, who had an outstanding NFL career and who now has a son who plays for the Buckeyes, and kicker Vlade Janakievski, who now owns and runs a deli near campus.

There are three others who, in my mind, stand alone after getting to know them:

Larry Zelina (RB)

Larry was part of the 1968 national championship team under Woody Hayes. He was the first former Ohio State player I met after taking my broadcasting gig. Larry could not have been any nicer about welcoming a new person to the Ohio State universe. I still recall his ear-to-ear smile and his vice-grip handshake. He was gone too soon, but I will always look back fondly on how my early days in Columbus included getting to know Larry.

John Hicks (OL)

I first came to know John while following the Ohio State teams of the 1970s. He not only collected serious hardware by the way of awards, but John almost broke down the door of the Heisman Trophy club, becoming a finalist for an award typically delivered to quarterbacks, running backs, and receivers. Sadly, I did not become acquainted with Big John until the final years of his life, but I was so impressed with how he rallied other former players when one of his teammates, Jack Tatum, was enduring some medical difficulties. Those who knew John better might agree that he, in so many ways, embodied what his coach, Woody Hayes, wanted in his players. John was also gone too soon, but he left a valuable impression on so many.

Archie Griffin (RB)

This man really needs no introduction for those who follow Ohio State or, for that matter, college football. Archie holds the distinction of being the only two-time winner of the Heisman Trophy, and he established numerous records during his career in Columbus. When people see Archie now, it's as if he won the second of his Heismans last week. He is treated with that degree of reverence and respect, and from personal experience, I would say it is because he is an award-winning person.

And now, on to basketball:

David Lighty (F)

One of the lesser-heralded members of the Thad Five recruiting group, Lighty became a player who could change a game both on offense and on defense. His play right before halftime against Tennessee kept Ohio State's Final Four hopes alive in 2007. He had one of his best shooting stretches in the first two rounds of the 2011 NCAA Tournament in his hometown of Cleveland. Thad Matta used to stump for a statue of Lighty to be placed at the Schottenstein Center for all of the intangibles that Lighty provided on and off the court. When Lighty missed most of the 2009 season with a foot injury, his absence was felt in a very big way.

Aaron Craft (PG)

He looked like someone had let their younger brother in the gym, but Craft set a tone right from his first game with his defense, energy, and effort. The way he would fly all over the court, dive on the floor for loose balls, track down opponents for steals, and just be a real pain in the rear end to anyone wearing a different uniform made Ohio State games during his time exciting. He was always good for interviews and always referred to you as "Mister." He had great manners, and his all-American looks also gave him a teen-idol type of appeal to the young female fans—and even some fans who had him by a few years. He was known so much for his defense, but Craft hit one of the biggest shots in recent history, a game-winning three-pointer against Iowa State in the NCAA Tournament in 2013. Then, in the very next game, with Arizona expecting him to repeat the feat, he dished the basketball to LaQuinton Ross, who nailed a game-winner against the Wildcats to clinch the Buckeyes a berth in the Elite Eight. When Craft's eligibility expired, it provided a sense of relief for rival Big Ten coaches such as Tom Izzo and John Beilein, who would constantly say it seemed like Craft had played for more than the allotted four years.

Jared Sullinger (F)

I became familiar with Jared because his brother, J.J., played at Ohio State earlier on, and I became acquainted with his father, Satch, a successful high school coach and administrator in Columbus. Jared, much like his AAU teammate Craft, showed great court savvy and could play the low-post game with other Big Ten big men right away. As much as he made an immediate impact on the court, Jared still displayed his easygoing type of charm off of the court that makes it a pleasant experience, even to this day, when you bump into him. I will always be flattered by the fact that Jared will, in his own humorous way, try to mimic what he thinks I sound like on the radio.

Jae'Sean Tate (F)

From the first time you saw him play for Ohio State, you became a fan because of his energy and effort. I recall when he was a freshman and Ohio State was playing North Carolina in Chicago, we were sitting right behind the bench—an awful vantage point for radio announcers, by the way—and he had to be taken out of the game by the coaches because he had played himself into a state of exhaustion! That would become something of a trademark for Tate. His energy was infectious at times and symbolized the positive trends that accompanied his tenure as a Buckeye. Having dealt with multiple shoulder injuries, Tate was able to deliver a game-winning bucket in the final seconds of a late-February contest at Penn State toward the end of his junior year. He was one of those guys you felt happiest for when the 2018 season resulted in an NCAA Tournament berth.

Je'Kel Foster (G)

A junior-college transfer from Mississippi, Je'Kel had committed to play at Ohio State while Jim O'Brien was still the head coach, but he played for Thad Matta instead. Years after the fact, Matta admitted that he was not familiar with Foster, but right away was working to get him to follow through and come to Columbus. Foster was another one of those young men who was easy to root for because of how hard he played and how polite he was. It was rumored that he was such a favorite of the head coach that, at times, teammates would call him Je'Kel Matta instead of Foster.

CHAPTER 11

20 YEARS IN THE BOOKS

It's like clockwork after every bowl trip, every NCAA Tournament run, every Michigan game, every momentous victory, and every last-minute triumph in either football or basketball. Those who know Paul Keels best pepper him with questions. They want to know anything and everything.

Did you have a good time? What did you get to do outside of work while you were there? (Usually, not much, because of time restraints.)

What was it like? Did the team celebrate like crazy in the locker room?

Do you get a national championship ring? (Yes.)

That had to be fun. What was your call at the end of the game?

And the one that never fails to be mentioned, of course: *Is there any way you could snag me tickets?*

Keels would not have it any other way, though. Friends, family members, and strangers on the street are all captivated by his tales and envious of his experiences. The moments he has enjoyed and the relationships he has built during his 20 years in Columbus have made work seem like the furthest thing from a chore.

In 2010 Keels missed a couple of games because of an emergency abdominal surgery. Ohio State had just jumped to the top of the national polls, and Jim Tressel and company trekked to Madison, Wisconsin, to defend their No. 1 ranking against the Badgers in a night game at raucous Camp Randall Stadium.

Meanwhile, Keels was in the hospital. Tressel called him the day the team departed for Wisconsin to wish him well. So, too, did Badgers head coach Bret Bielema. The two got to know each other through a Wisconsin radio announcer, and they continue to trade texts a couple times a year. Ohio State lost that game 31–18, as Wisconsin sprinted out to a three-touchdown advantage early in the second quarter.

Keels has made countless connections with coaches during his two decades behind the mic in Columbus. He developed a bond with former Minnesota coach Glen Mason and former Indiana coach Kevin Wilson.

Mason, who, it was believed, quietly coveted the Ohio State coaching gig, would prattle on about his admiration for Woody Hayes and Earle Bruce. Keels has also enjoyed his chats with Northwestern boss Pat Fitzgerald about recruiting in Ohio. Fitzgerald would occasionally do interviews with the Ohio State announcing crew while he worked out. Keels learned about former Northwestern coach Randy Walker's fondness for Skyline Chili and of Bob Ferguson, the stout Ohio State fullback who was a unanimous All-America selection in 1960 and 1961. Both Walker and Ferguson hailed from Troy, Ohio.

Former Michigan coach Brady Hoke told Keels he would listen to the Ohio State broadcasts of football or basketball games whenever he was traveling around or recruiting in Ohio. Hoke grew up in Dayton, and he always made sure to devote time to Keels and Lachey on the interview circuit at Big Ten media days in Chicago in the summer. Lloyd Carr did the same.

I know that will gnash the teeth of Ohio State fans.

Kirk Ferentz started coaching at Iowa in 1999, the year after Keels relocated to Columbus. Keels said it's easy to see how the four-time Big Ten Coach of the Year has lasted so long in Iowa City.

When you meet him and you see him every year, he truly seems happy to see you.

When Jerry Kill was the head man at Minnesota, he said at the close of an interview with Keels and Jim Lachey, "Hey, wouldn't that be nice if Ohio State and Minnesota met in the Big Ten Championship Game? If that happens, I'll buy you guys dinner in Indianapolis." Keels and Lachey are still waiting to make a reservation for three at St. Elmo Steak House downtown.

Tracy Claeys replaced Kill as head coach of the Golden Gophers after health issues forced Kill to step down. In 2015, when Claeys led Minnesota into Columbus to challenge the No. 1–ranked Buckeyes, he had someone drive him to the Woody Hayes Athletic Center, a mile north of Ohio Stadium. Claeys, appreciative of legendary coaches, had his picture taken as he stood next to the Woody Hayes statue outside of the building. Coaches can be awestruck, too.

Kyle Flood, the head coach at Rutgers from 2012 to 2015, was a big fan of Lachey. Flood spent about two decades as an offensive-line coach at various schools before he latched on with the Scarlet Knights. Lachey starred as an offensive tackle at Ohio State and in the NFL with the Washington Redskins. So when Rutgers traveled to Columbus for a matchup in 2014—Rutgers' first year in the Big Ten—Keels, Lachey, and producer Skip Mosic were set to interview Flood. First, however, Flood had the team's sports information director hand him his cell phone so the head coach could take a selfie with Lachey.

I don't think you would see many head coaches do that.

Lachey arrives at the stadium on Saturdays or at the airport on a travel day as if he were in the starting lineup. He spreads a genuine excitement and passion, even though he has not played for Ohio State in more than 30 years. He is still grateful and thrilled to be involved with the football program. Lachey has access to closed practices, so he gets to know the players and the coaches, the schemes and the strategies, which allows him to present a perspective on the broadcasts that no one else can rival. Keels said Lachey prepares for the games as a play-by-play announcer would, which is rare for an analyst. He studies his charts that include players' names, numbers, and statistics.

*When you physically see him, you would never know that this
was a guy who was an All-Pro offensive lineman who played
on a Super Bowl championship team. He is one of those down-
to-Earth guys, and he is seemingly always in a good mood.*

Both Keels and Lachey have their own set of brothers, but they have
worked so closely together for so long, that they often feel like brothers
themselves.

*We do often finish each others' sentences—or say the same
words at the same time.*

In Keels' house, there is a closet with a big box full of old cassette
tapes. The Big Ten Network asked him for some audio material from
the 1992 Final Four, when he called Cincinnati's matchup against
Michigan's Fab Five. It's not often that Keels dusts off the cassettes and
listens to his calls. His voice has chronicled every impactful moment of
Ohio State football and basketball over the last two decades, but it's still a
bit awkward for him to hear it on replays, especially ones from long ago.

*The sound of your own voice irritates you as it is. Then when
you hear it from when you were younger, it's even a little more
alarming. It sounds a little higher-pitched, or maybe it's the
cassette tape quality. Sometimes you need to do that, though,
just from a self-critiquing standpoint. How did you do it then?
What are you doing differently now? What are you not doing?*

Regardless of what Keels thinks of his own bellowing sound, he will
forever be associated with national championships and Final Fours, with
unforgettable touchdowns and desperation three-pointers. And that is
something he still can't quite wrap his head around, even 20 years into
the job in Columbus.

It is weird. It's flattering, it's complimentary, but it is weird. You don't do it for the recognition. You do it because it's what you enjoy doing.

Keels was 41 years old when he accepted the Ohio State job. He had moved away from his comfort zone in Cincinnati a couple of times already. He had worked at the network level for a while. He was both thrilled and relieved when he returned to his hometown and called Cincinnati Bearcats games. He had chased a broadcasting position with the Tampa Bay Rays when the expansion franchise joined Major League Baseball in time for the 1998 season. He interviewed for the play-by-play role, and he was told he was one of four final candidates for the gig. He did not get the job, though, and he decided that he would direct his focus to football and basketball.

When the Ohio State job became available, he knew it was a forever job. This would not be something he would accept while still keeping an eye on the ever-changing list of openings. This was it. Keels knew it was not a springboard to something greater. This *was* the something greater. It was his home state, just a two-hour trek north on I-71 from his hometown. He was already familiar with the area, having visited his relatives in Columbus so often as a kid. This was a football program that would treat him to the biggest games and the household names, a program that stayed in the spotlight and always kept things interesting. There would be no more 81–0 losses to Penn State, no more winless seasons. It was a basketball program with a rich history, too, and a promise of potential.

When he first stepped into the broadcast booth in Columbus, his voice described the play of the No. 1 football team in the country and an eventual Final Four hoops squad. Over the last 20 years, his iconic baritone has narrated every fateful moment.

I thought, "These kinds of jobs do not open very often, and I would like to be part of making sure it does not open again for a long time."

ACKNOWLEDGMENTS

This doesn't happen without the writing talents of Zack Meisel. The experience is made better by working with a true pro. Thanks Zack for doing so much of the heavy lifting!

—Paul Keels